FREE TO ACT

DEAN L. LARSEN

BOOKCRAFT
Salt Lake City, Utah

Library of Congress Catalog Card Number: 89-62313

ISBN 0-88494-712-2

First Printing, 1989

Printed in the United States of America

For behold, ye are free; ye are permitted to act for yourselves; for behold, God hath given unto you a knowledge and he hath made you free.

—Helaman 14:30

Contents

Preface

Those who have known the gospel best throughout history have had the conviction that it can have its most powerful and far-reaching effects in the people's lives when they comprehend and practice it in its simplest form. They had great faith that if people would believe in Jesus Christ and the fundamentals of his gospel plan and were then free to apply their faith and understanding as light and intelligence would guide them to do, the condition of their lives would inevitably improve. It would expand and flower in the full range of their experience.

Over the centuries this spiritual phenomenon has been witnessed repeatedly. It is as though when the gospel is accepted on those terms a wellspring of incentive and creativity is tapped which cannot be restrained so long as the light persists.

These extraordinary bursts of human progress and enlightenment that have accompanied the various dispensations of the gospel have not occurred because all of the details of procedure and application were perceived by an enlightened few and then prescribed by them for the people. The magic has been contained in the irrepressible power that faith in Jesus Christ and his gospel engenders in individual souls. Once that light and power have been kindled, a spontaneous blossoming occurs that reaches in almost every direction. This is the miracle of the Lord's plan. To trust in it requires great faith and conviction. It can touch people in almost any set of circumstances, and if then they carefully nurture the light they will immediately begin to improve those circumstances; not because a detailed course of procedure is marked out for them, but because they will perceive for themselves, by the divine light that is within them, what must be done.

It is also apparent that people can be conditioned away from this divine power. As they increasingly turn to men's devices and the arm of flesh, the light subsides; spiritual darkness ensues, and the problems of the world eventually engulf them.

As one contemplates the magnificent promise made by the Lord to those who seek one day to be exalted in his presence, it is clear that those who achieve that status must have grown to a high level of personal accountability—an accountability born of internal impetus to do the right things for the right reasons. No one can be programmed or manipulated into eternal life by the will or compelling force of another. As Lehi said, one must receive the redeeming power of the Savior's infinite atonement and then, knowing good from evil, must be free to act for oneself and not be acted upon, save by the consequences of eternal laws (see 2 Nephi 2:26–27).

Samuel the Lamanite voiced the same conviction:

"And now remember, remember, my brethren, that whosoever perisheth, perisheth unto himself; and whosoever doeth iniquity, doeth it unto himself; for behold, ye are free; ye are permitted to act for yourselves; for behold, God hath given unto you a knowledge and he hath made you free.

"He hath given unto you that ye might know good from evil, and he hath given unto you that ye might choose life or death; and ye can do good and be restored unto that which is good, or have that which is good restored unto you; or ye can do evil, and have that which is evil restored unto you." (Helaman 14:30–31.)

A deep conviction of the importance of personal accountability has prompted the pages that follow. This book is not an official Church publication, and I assume full responsibility for the views it expresses. They reflect my own perception of things as supported by my understanding of the revealed word of God and his eternal plan for his children. They are shared here with the hope that they might stimulate greater insight and understanding regarding the remarkable plan of progress marked out for us by a loving Heavenly Father, with an emphasis upon the part that we ourselves must play.

We have been made knowledgeable, and we have been made free; we must act for ourselves. The blessings of eternal life are ours to claim. We will be accountable for the results.

CHAPTER ONE

Accountability and Human Progress

We live in a time when the most fundamental principles pertaining to human happiness and progress are being challenged. Decency, honor, integrity, and morality are being discounted in favor of self-gratification and expediency. Freedom and self-accountability are being bartered for regulation, regimentation, and programmed security. It is important that we periodically assess the effect of these developments upon the course of our lives. Latter-day Saints should understand that mortal life was purposefully designed to place us in circumstances wherein we can be individually tested and wherein, by the exercise of the agency God has given us, we can determine what our future possibilities will be. Understanding this, Lehi, the Book of Mormon prophet, said to his son Jacob: "Wherefore, men are free according to the flesh; and all things are given them which are expedient unto man.

And they are free to choose liberty and eternal life, through the great Mediator of all men, or to choose captivity and death.'' (2 Nephi 2:27.)

He further explained that men "have become free forever, knowing good from evil; to act for themselves and not to be acted upon, save it be by the punishment of the law . . . according to the commandments which God hath given" (2 Nephi 2:26).

The Lord confirmed to Joseph Smith that he had raised up and inspired "wise men" to establish the United States Constitution (see D&C 101:80) so that "every man may act in doctrine and principle pertaining to futurity, according to the moral agency which I have given unto him, that every man may be accountable. . . ." The Lord referred to these essential provisions in the Constitution as "just and holy principles." (D&C 101:77–78.)

In the Constitution the Lord established a fine balance of freedoms and restraints. Anticipating the time when this balance would be in jeopardy, he said, with respect to the constitutional law: "And as pertaining to law of man, whatsoever is more or less than this, cometh of evil. I, the Lord God, make you free, therefore ye are free indeed; and the law also maketh you free. Nevertheless, when the wicked rule the people mourn." (D&C 98:7–9.)

The essential freedoms to which the Lord alludes in these important revelations are necessary in order to provide the highest prospects for human development. For those Latter-day Saints in the United States they have traditionally been so much a part of the regular environment that we are not always consciously aware of them. We don't take inventory of them each day to see whether they are still there, although perhaps we should. In some respects they are taken for granted because they have become so much a part of the fiber of life.

We seem to become more specifically aware of these qualities of life when we feel we are being deprived of them in one way or another. At these times we feel the inclination to object to and resist such encroachments into our freedoms. It is only when we are shocked by their aggregate effect that we become alarmed.

It is important that we understand the critical nature of these incursions into our basic freedoms. They represent a threat as vital as a threat to such natural processes as breathing or movement. They affect not only our opportunities in this life but our eternal possibilities as well.

By our very endowment as children of an Eternal Father, we have had implanted within our souls the urgency to be free. It is natural for us to want to be accountable for our own fates, because there is a whispering within us confirming that this accountability is absolutely essential to the attainment of our eternal destiny. If we understand how important this freedom is, we will struggle to preserve it as though our very lives are at stake; for, indeed, these qualities are life—they are the very essence of living.

The Declaration of Independence was simply an expression of men who would not tolerate the encroachment of restrictive forces into those areas of their lives wherein they knew that freedom was imperative. Their declaration was an acknowledgment and a warning that governmental power had reached and exceeded certain limits to which the signers were not willing to yield. Their statement is eloquent and inspiring. Their feeling and commitment were no more conclusive than our own should be. Their expectations have carried through the years to us. This is not so much a result of the documents they produced—profound and inspired as they were and still are—as it is the result of the fact that these same desires and commitments have continued in honest men's hearts through all the intervening generations.

The preserving and enforcing powers which we by custom attribute to the Constitution and the Bill of Rights are not so much in the documents themselves as they are in the powers within men and women who believe in and are committed to the principles that motivated the producers of the original documents.

The existence of laws, regulations, and procedures has never been sufficient in itself to compel men to obedience. Productive obedience comes through the exercise of free will. Albert E. Bowen said, "It is a truism that no law is any better than the people who administer it. Howsoever well framed a law may be or however worthy its purpose, it can degenerate into utter futility unless wisely administered by those sympathetic with its purpose." (Gospel Doctrine Course of Study, second half of 1946, Deseret Sunday School Union.)

Today we need not so much fear that men may change the Constitution as that they may change their hearts, their expectations. This does not diminish in any way the need for the inspired guidelines in the national constitution. These must remain intact. But the Constitution as a document will generate little power if people are not sympathetic with its purpose and if they do not understand and value the principles which undergird it. These principles, as we have already said, are fundamental to eternal progress. We cannot afford to be complacent about them.

As was the case in another time prior to the creation of this earth on which we now live, an all-out attempt is being made to obscure our vision and to content us with settling for a stifling, imposed security. We are told in the scriptural record that on that earlier occasion, fully one-third of all the hosts who contemplated the challenges of mortal life allowed themselves to be deluded into thinking that there were acceptable alternatives to the essential risks that accompany the exercise of agency and free will (see Moses 4:1–4; Abraham 3:27–28; Revelation 12:4). The price paid by those earlier unfortunates is beyond comprehension. The stakes are no less consequential in the current struggle, and the source of the present confusion is the same as it was in that earlier day. Satan's determination to lull us away into a sense of carnal security, cheat our souls of our highest potential, and carefully lead us down to a hell of frustration and inertia is as great now as it ever was (see 2 Nephi 28:21).

As I contemplate the erosion which is occurring in personal freedoms in many parts of the world, I have concluded that the counterforces which must be generated in order to preserve an environment of freedom cannot be legislated into existence. Nor will they be the product of oratory or of public demonstration, although these may serve some useful purpose.

Probably the most powerful influence at work today to secure to us our heritage of freedom and accountability is that which emanates from the lives of individuals who understand and apply the principles that relate to eternal progress. This combined influence is among the greatest forces on the earth. We must not only ensure that honest and honorable people are elected to public office, as the Lord has advised (see D&C 98:10); we need also to see to it that they represent an honest and honorable, freedom-seeking constituency.

Likely the most powerful political action I can take today is to see that my own house is in order. I do not suggest that we not become involved in the regular political processes; our expectations and views should be registered in the public forum. But shrewd politics and politicians will not save us. Unless the people themselves retain a vibrant desire to be free—to be unencumbered by unnecessary and debilitating regulation and manipulation—and unless they understand and practice the principles which give life to those freedoms, we have little reason to hope that they will endure. When the people are conditioned to accept dependency and regulation and to cease valuing independence and self-accountability, they are vulnerable to the forces that destroy freedom. When loyalty is measured only on the basis of one's willingness to conform to a regulatory authority, or when righteousness is judged primarily by the degree to which one responds to programmed, regimented activity, an environment is created within which essential freedoms decline. The resulting tragedy not only affects the mortal potential of man. It also has a profound effect on his eternal possibilities.

Regimented behavior is incapable of producing the level of spiritual development required to qualify one for eternal life. A necessary range of freedom and accountability is essential to one's spiritual development. To ensure that development a person must, with an understanding of correct principles and an intrinsic desire to apply them, be motivated within himself to do many good things of his own free will; for, as the revelation says, the power is in him wherein he is an agent unto himself (see D&C 58:26–29).

Our need is to have a deep concern for preserving an environment which fosters a spirit of freedom and self-determination. We cannot ignore the need for carefully ordered structure and procedure for group action within government or within any other effective organization. This discussion is not an argument for anarchy. It underlines, however, the need for careful balance between that which is programmed for the group and that which is reserved for the conscience and incentive of the individual. It is a concern which may touch any sector of our lives—in matters of politics and economy, for example, as well as in religion and morals.

It would appear that the same balance of freedom and restraint spoken of by the Lord with respect to the Constitution and national government has application to many other areas of our lives. It can apply to relationships within families and communities, and it cannot be ignored in our assignments of responsibility within the Church. I have often pondered the term "unrighteous dominion" as it was used in the cautionary expressions of Joseph Smith which appear in Doctrine and Covenants section 121. There we are warned "that it is the nature and disposition of almost all men [and I presume we could add 'almost all *women*'], as soon as they get a little authority, as they suppose, they will immediately begin to exercise unrighteous dominion" (D&C 121:39).

How do men, or women, unrighteously dominate the lives of others? How can the principle of balanced freedoms and restraints apply to our relationships within our families and within our Church responsibilities? Is there reason to be cautious in this area of our lives? Remember that the Lord said with respect to national government that anything "more or less" than the ideal balance he had provided "cometh of evil," obviously meaning also that it would have an evil effect and would be detrimental to human progress.

In March 1940 President J. Reuben Clark made some remarks on behalf of the First Presidency in a meeting with general auxiliary leaders. He recognized the need for restraint, even within the framework of the Church and its design to help its members perfect their lives. Then he said: "The work of the Church in all fields is standing in grave danger of being regimented down to the minutest detail. The result of that will be that not only will all the initiative be crushed out but that all opportunity for the working of the Spirit will be eliminated. The Church has not been built on that principle. . . . It will be a mistake to assume that there is not a great and sufficient reservoir of initiative in the Church to carry on if that reservoir be drawn upon. Such initiative existed in the past; it exists now." (From a memorandum of the First Presidency to general auxiliary leaders, dated March 29, 1940.)

In April 1979 in his concluding remarks at the general conference of the Church, President Kimball said:

> The basic decisions needed for us to move forward, as a people, must be made by the individual members of the Church. . . . The major strides which must be made by the Church will follow upon the major strides to be made by us as individuals. . . . Our individual spiritual growth is the key to major numerical growth in the kingdom. . . . Only as we see clearly the responsibility of each individual and the role of families and the home can we properly understand that the priesthood quorums and the auxiliary organizations, even wards and

stakes, exist primarily to help members live the gospel in the home. (*Ensign,* May 1979, pp. 82–83.)

President Kimball enlarged upon this theme as he spoke to Regional Representatives and General Authorities in the seminar for Regional Representatives on October 5, 1979. On that occasion he said; "We see ourselves as positioning our people so that the Latter-day Saints can give greater attention to family life, can focus more on simple and basic things, can render more Christian service, and can have greater effectiveness in all these things—through the process of simplification, scheduling, proper priorities, and by honoring the priesthood line."

Programmed behavior and performance may have some temporary value as a defense against overt negative behavior, since it fills one's time with "constructive" activity. It has never been demonstrated, however, that programmed behavior, even when it is correct, has the power to lift one to the level of self-motivation and commitment associated with celestial life. There is an essential element of individual freedom and initiative that must be present for this type of development to occur. To argue that people generally cannot be entrusted with this kind of freedom is to argue against the very purpose of mortal life.

As the freedom for unrestricted development is enhanced, the possibilities for failure are also increased. That is one of the jeopardies of the Lord's plan. The risk factor is great. The ideal cannot be achieved otherwise. Celestial attainment can be reached in no other environment. In such a system there are likely to be more "called" than "chosen" (see D&C 121:34). Such was the anticipation from the beginning.

Inspired leaders today are reconfirming with us the fact that there is no ultimate safety in programmed security wherein others assume accountability for our direction and performance. I appreciate a statement made by Albert Payne to that effect:

> A distinguishing feature of Church organization lies in its balance of authority and individual rights. Priesthood is a brotherhood, and in its operation the highest capacities of man—his capacity to act as a free agent, and his capacity to be spiritual—must be respected and enlarged. Leaders invite, persuade, encourage, and recommend in a spirit of gentleness and meekness. Members respond freely as the Spirit guides. Only this kind of response has moral value. Fear and force have no place in the kingdom because they do not produce moral actions and are contrary to God's gift of free agency. (From an unpublished document; used with permission.)

It is the role of the Church to teach the gospel of salvation and redemption through Jesus Christ, to administer the sacred, saving ordinances by proper authority, to provide the basic order within which essential group action can occur, and to preserve purity and correctness of belief and practice. Those who insist that the Church provide for every contingency and need are as much in error as their counterparts who demand that government intervene in every aspect of our lives. In both instances the balance between "more" and "less" is destroyed, with resultant detriment to human progress.

When any agency affecting our lives is invited or required to step beyond its proper bounds, opportunity for progress is hindered. Freedom and spontaneity within the regular daily transactions of family and community life, when guided by an understanding of gospel principles, are necessary in order for us to prove ourselves and to achieve celestial qualities.

These are essential truths which press us to make our lives better by our own initiative and by our own efforts. They make no unconditional promises.

At the same time, our obedience to them preserves for us the elements of life which make individual progress possible. They make life purposeful and keep it full of promise. They lead to eternal progress. Humanity cannot fulfill its destiny when these truths are disregarded and abused.

CHAPTER TWO

*Accountability
and the Plan
of Salvation*

*T*here are three principal facets of the plan of salvation that have a direct bearing upon personal accountability. One of these has to do with the provisions made for us by the Godhead and over which we do not have control or which we cannot initiate. I refer to such provisions as the infinite atonement of Christ with all of its effects; the spiritual gifts, including the ministrations of the Holy Spirit; the saving ordinances and the priesthood authority necessary to perform them; the earth itself and the organization of the Church; the laws and principles embodied in the gospel of Jesus Christ.

Another facet of the plan of salvation directly related to personal accountability has to do with the personal attributes or inherent qualities that each of us possesses as a child of God. These would include our intelligence; our will or agency—the capacity to make choices; and our capacity to respond to spiritual forces that emanate from God, which some have identified with the conscience.

A third related facet of the plan of salvation is environmental in nature. It is concerned with the circumstances we encounter here in earth life, where laws of cause and effect are free to operate and where so many alternatives are available to us. It is an environment ideally suited for testing and proving.

Personal accountability is affected by all of these aspects of the plan. It is very important for us to understand that, without the condition of personal accountability, the plan of salvation cannot operate successfully.

Perhaps it would be helpful to define accountability. I do not believe that the standard dictionary definition encompasses all that the Lord ascribes to this condition or quality in human beings. There is a difference between accountability and responsibility. Responsibility relates to a set of duties or expectations that may be placed upon us by others or by ourselves. Responsibility places one in a position to be accountable.

Accountability has to do with one's exercising his own will to make decisions and follow a course of conduct. It implies self-initiative and a measure of self-reliance, but it requires more than the ability to act for one's self. It must be guided by a knowledge of true principles. Accountability is heightened by the confirmation of the Holy Spirit as to what is right and wrong. In fact, to act in matters of great importance without this confirmation is to act unaccountably.

The condition of personal accountability is essential to the operation of eternal justice and judgment.

The Lord has said that one should enter into the covenants associated with the saving ordinances only when one has begun to be accountable (see D&C 29:46–47). In fact, we are advised that if, for some reason, an individual is limited or handicapped in such a way that he cannot function as an accountable person, and if he cannot be held accountable for willful choices affecting his behavior, he should not enter into covenants that require such accountability. He will not be judged on the same basis as an accountable person until such time as it is possible for him to function without the limitations. (See D&C 29:49–50; 134:12; Moroni 8:22.)

To the degree to which one becomes more fully accountable, he becomes more like God. Note the expression made with regard to Adam and Eve when they had partaken of the fruit of the tree of knowledge of good and evil. "And I, the Lord God, said unto mine Only Begotten: Behold, the man is become as one of us to know good and evil" (Moses 4:28). Such knowledge is essential to accountability, and with this knowledge men become "free . . . to act for themselves and not to be acted upon, save it be by the punishment of the law at the great and last day, according to the commandments which God hath given" (2 Nephi 2:26).

The condition of accountability, therefore, is not to be avoided if one is to progress. It is, indeed, essential to progression in the Lord's plan of salvation.

It could be said that to the degree to which we attempt to avoid or escape from accountability ourselves, or to act in such a way that we inhibit the accountability of others, we interfere with the plan of progress.

As knowledge and experience increase and as spiritual enlightenment is enhanced, the level of accountability is raised. The degree to which an individual is expected to assert himself in the pursuit of good works is broadened.

Following are some suggestions on how one might act in a more accountable way and thereby increase his opportunities for eternal progress.

1. *Face difficult decisions*

All of us are at times faced with decisions that have a profound effect on the course of our lives or upon the lives of those with whom we have the greatest influence. When we face such decisions, we may feel a reluctance to commit ourselves to a course of action. Sometimes there is the temptation to transfer the decision to someone else and thereby escape the accountability ourselves.

When I was serving as a young bishop with only limited experience in Church leadership, and lacking much in the way of practical experience as well, I was approached by an elderly couple in my ward. They were old enough to be my grandparents. For years they had successfully farmed a piece of ground. They had been blessed in many ways and had reared a fine family. None of the children had showed an inclination to follow in their father's footsteps as a farmer. Increasing age and declining health had brought the couple to a point of decision as to what should be done with their farm. They were reluctant to have it pass from their hands after so many years of labor and careful improvement. The children could not agree on a plan of action. Some wished to keep the farm in the family and lease it for an income to be shared among the family members; others didn't care what decision was made.

One Sunday afternoon the couple appeared at my office in the ward chapel and asked to consult with me.

They explained their dilemma and their reluctance to make a decision that might divide the family and jeopardize their own welfare for the remaining years of their lives. "We have come to you, Bishop," the old gentleman said, "to ask you to find out for us what the Lord wants us to do."

I was humbled by the sincere trust that the couple were willing to place with me, but I sensed that the decision they were attempting to lay upon me and upon the Lord was not ours to make. I counseled them in the best way I could, tried to help them weigh the alternatives, and then recommended that they prayerfully reach a decision themselves and ask their family to sustain them. They left my office in great disappointment, making it quite clear to me that they felt I was not fulfilling my responsibility as a bishop.

I believe that whenever we try to avoid the accountability for decisions such as this in our own lives, we fail to understand one of the purposes for which we came into mortal life. It is altogether proper and wise to seek the best possible counsel before making crucial decisions. It is sometimes necessary to seek inspiration through prayer and fasting. But I am convinced that the Lord does not want us to abdicate the accountability for the final choices we make. And I believe he honors those choices when they are made in the proper way. If we refuse to accept such accountability, we jeopardize our possibilities for progress and thwart the purpose for which we were allowed to come to the earth.

2. *Don't rob others of the opportunity to be accountable*

In our relationships with others we must be careful not to prevent them from acting accountably. This is especially significant when we are given positions of leadership or responsibility which place others under our charge. The Lord's concern about this sensitive area in human relations called forth the excellent counsel we find in section 121 of the Doctrine and Covenants. There the Lord warns us against exercising unrighteous dominion. He cautions against compulsion and controls. The proper way to influence the behavior of others, he says, is "by persuasion, by long-suffering, by gentleness and meekness, and love unfeigned; by kindness, and pure knowledge, which shall greatly enlarge the soul without hypocrisy, and without guile" (D&C 121:41–42).

In the next verse the Lord acknowledges the need to occasionally reprove with sharpness when inspired to do so, but counsels that even this reproof should be delivered and followed up in a spirit of love.

Manipulation, programming, and regimentation are destructive to personal accountability. It does not matter how benevolent the motive of a parent or leader who compels his children or his subordinates to follow his precise prescriptions. The motive does not prevent unfortunate results from occurring and the development of a conditioned dependency.

Significant to this observation is the acknowledgment that we grow into accountability. As infants we come into mortal life in a state of innocence (see D&C 93:38). Parents are made responsible for teaching their children about the purpose of life. They are to teach their children to pray and to walk uprightly before the Lord. They are to be models of righteousness. (See D&C 68:25.) All of this is to be done in order that the children can be brought to a state of accountability wherein they can become liable to the operation of eternal law and justice in consequence of their own will-directed conduct.

One may willingly submit himself to the requirements, controls, regulations, and domination of another in the performance of good deeds, but until he does those deeds of his own free will (see D&C 58:27) he does not experience the essential intrinsic development of personal qualities and values. The Lord has warned us against doing only those things that we are commanded to do (see D&C 58:29). In so doing we become puppets, acting by the will of another.

It was for this reason that President John Taylor once made the following declaration subsequent to an experience in which someone had attempted to compel him unrighteously.

"I was not born a slave! I cannot, will not be a slave. I would not be a slave to God! I'd be His servant, friend, His son. I'd go at His behest; but would not be His slave. I'd rather be extinct than be a slave. His friend I feel I am, and He is mine:—a slave! The manacles would pierce my very bones—the clanking chains would grate upon my soul—a poor, lost, servile, crawling wretch to lick the dust and fawn and smile upon the thing who gave the lash! . . . But stop! I'm God's free man: I will not, cannot be a slave! Living, I'll be free here, or free in life above—free with the Gods, for they are free." (B. H. Roberts, *The Life of John Taylor,* Bookcraft, 1963, p. 424.)

I remember well an incident that occurred years ago involving my son. He is the father of three children himself now; and I must add that he is a better father in many ways than I was. I suspect he would not remember this incident—even so, I think he would not mind my sharing it here.

He must have been seven or eight years old at the time. We lived in a house that was located at the end of a dead-end street that extended for about a half block off one of the well-traveled thoroughfares. Around the corner from our house and about two blocks up the through-street was a small corner grocery store that was usually open seven days a week.

My son and I had had some conversations about the responsibility for using money wisely. I had felt that my counsel with him on this matter had been well received and to good effect. We had also had a number of discussions with our little family about the importance of the Sabbath day.

Then one Sunday afternoon when we had returned to our home following Church services, my son and several of his friends paraded into our living room where I was reading. The lady who lived down the street from us had just rewarded the boys with a twenty-five-cent piece for each of them for some yard work they had helped her with the day before. They proudly showed me their quarters and announced that they were going to walk down to the corner grocery store and buy some candy.

I caught myself just in time to stifle the inclination to say abruptly, "No, not on Sunday!" Instead, I reminded my son about our talks concerning the use of money and called his attention to our family's policy about not going to the stores on Sunday. He was obviously troubled and a little chagrined at my response in the presence of his friends. I could tell that he was caught in a situation that was a little difficult for him. It was a good opportunity, I felt, to let him make his own decision. "Well," I said, "you know what we have talked about concerning the use of money, and you know how Mother and I feel about keeping the Sabbath, so you decide what you ought to do."

The boys left our home and went out to the lawn in front of the house. I stood by a window where I would not be observed, and watched. For a time the boys sat on the grass in a discussion that I could not overhear. I concluded that they were not going to the store, and I was complimenting myself on the wisdom that I had used in handling the situation.

Suddenly all the boys got to their feet and started down the street. They rounded the corner and were obviously headed for the store. I was not only disappointed, I was incensed. I determined not to let my son go through with his obvious decision, and more than that, I was going to let him know in no uncertain terms how I felt about it.

I searched for the keys to our automobile, fearful that the boys would reach the store before I could intercept them. I backed the car out of our driveway and drove quickly to the intersection with the through-street. As I was turning the corner toward the store, I saw the boys. They were within a hundred yards of their destination. They had stopped and were apparently having another discussion. I stopped and eased back into our street far enough that I would not be obvious to them. In a moment I could tell that a decision had been made, and my son was walking alone toward our house while the other boys went on to the store.

I backed my car into our driveway and pulled under the carport to wait for my son. In a moment he came through the adjoining lot where there was a prune orchard. He was taking a shortcut. He kicked at the clods of dirt as he came to our fence, and, without any comment to me as he saw me in the car, he entered the house and was soon engaged in an activity with his sisters.

I realized that in my urgency to have my will obeyed I had almost cheated him of the opportunity to make an important decision for himself. I learned an important lesson that day about allowing people to be account-able.

3. *Demonstrate accountability by doing many good things of your own free will*

A truly accountable person will not require direction in every act of Christian service. Neither will he require acknowledgment or reward for all the good he does. In his desire to emulate the Savior he will "do many [good] things of [his] own free will" (D&C 58:27).

I once drove a considerable distance to attend a testi-monial for a friend who was leaving his home for a new position in another section of the country. The winter weather was threatening and roads were hazardous. It should have been easy to excuse myself from the obliga-tion. I had been given no part to play in the proceedings, and it was unlikely that I would be recognized in the throng that would undoubtedly gather. But this man had reached out his hand to me at a critical time and had touched my life, and my life had changed as a result. I felt compelled to go and join the others in paying him this honor.

The community in which the man had lived was a small one. He had never drawn about him much of the world's goods. The little business he had operated could have been profitable enough, but he was too interested in people to be much concerned with the profit motive. He was always available but never demanding. There was nothing ostentatious about his charity. Most of us had learned to take him very much for granted, and it is unlikely that he ever would have been given any public honor until his burial day, had not his unexpected leaving brought us to remember how important his influence and friendship had been to us. The gathering on this night was the spontaneous expression of our love and sense of loss.

This same spontaneity characterized the testimonial meeting. As we entered the hall in which the gathering was to be held, we were asked to sign our names on slips of paper which were then folded and placed in a cardboard box. When the large crowd was seated and the honored guest had taken his place on the stand, we sang a song, a prayer was offered, and the chairman arose to announce the proceedings. He pointed to the cardboard box which was now on the rostrum. Names would be drawn from the box, he explained, and those who were chosen in this manner would be asked to represent all who were present in their expressions of love and gratitude for our departing friend.

One by one the names were drawn. As the hour passed, a procession of unrehearsed speakers filed to the podium and there unfolded a legacy of selfless service that this man had given. In absorbing the drama of the occasion, each one must have become sensitive to the goodness that had reflected from him and had become mirrored in one way or another in our own lives.

As the meeting drew to a close, the name of a local physician was extracted from the box. For many years the good doctor had lived as a neighbor to our honored friend. He had recently returned to his home following treatment in another state for what had proved to be a near-fatal illness. He earnestly addressed himself to the gathering. For many years, he explained, he had contemplated the parallels in his own life and that of his neighbor. From his point of view, each of them had been preeminently involved in service to others. He told of leaving his home to make professional calls at hours both early and late and of frequently encountering our friend departing on what seemed to be similar errands of compassion. It was at these times, the doctor said, that he felt particularly drawn to his neighbor in a fellowship of service.

At this point the speaker paused involuntarily, and his voice became touched with emotion. Making reference to his recent illness, he related how he had left this same community several months before, not knowing whether he would ever return. No farewell testimonial had been held in his honor. He confessed that he had been a little disturbed by the obvious inequity in the attentions shown to him and to his neighbor, particularly in light of the service that both had given to the people of the community. Tonight, however, it had occurred to him why this was so.

With all of the apparent parallels between his life and that of his friend, there was one profound difference that set them apart in the eyes of their fellows. For all of his services, the doctor pointed out, he had collected a fee. That was the difference. He had not realized until now how much his fees had cost him.

Those of us who knew the good doctor and had been the recipients of his kindly ministrations realized that his self-deprecation was unjustified. But he succeeded in these dramatic circumstances in imparting a lesson that most of us will not soon forget.

4. *Be willing to accept difficulties without blaming God*

One of the provisions made for us by our Heavenly Father in his plan for our eternal progress was the nature of the environment into which we come in mortal life. Life on earth is ideally suited to test us and prove us. Laws of cause and effect operate freely. There is opposition in all things. The conditions are designed to bring about the maturation and development essential to the progress of man in this mortal phase of his existence. Earth life is filled with risks. It provides no guarantee for safe passage. It expands our prospects for developing personal accountability.

No one passes through mortality without occasionally experiencing disappointment, heartache, and perhaps even tragedy. Once in a while, for reasons known only to him, the Lord responds to our pleading and our prayers of faith and miraculously rescues us from a trial or difficulty. Generally, however, he expects us to cope with them. He trusts that our faith in him, our understanding of life's true purpose, and the infinite promises associated with his atonement for us will sustain us and enable us to endure. We act accountably when we accept these conditions and manifest our willingness to comply with the Lord's plan.

Too frequently we hear accusations against God for bringing difficulties or calamities upon people. Or we torture ourselves with the thought that God is punishing us because of our imperfections. Or the relief from trials fails to come despite our earnest, persistent prayers. Such thoughts must have crossed the mind of Joseph Smith as he was confined for months in a dark prison cell in Liberty, Missouri, while his family and friends in the Church were being driven and abused. It is well for us to remember the Lord's response to the Prophet's appeal for relief and for an understanding of the purpose in all of the difficulty: "Know thou, my son, that all these things shall give thee experience, and shall be for thy good" (D&C 122:7).

When burdens are lifted or when apparently inevitable consequences of illness or accident miraculously pass us by, we have cause for the deepest gratitude and thanksgiving. But when we are expected to endure, it should not be with an accusing spirit. The Apostle Paul once wrote to the Saints in Rome, "For I reckon that the sufferings of this present time are not worthy to be compared with the glory which shall be revealed in us" (Romans 8:18).

And the Lord said to the Prophet Joseph: "My son, peace be unto thy soul; thine adversity and thine afflictions shall be but a small moment. And then, if thou endure it well, God shall exalt thee on high; thou shalt triumph over all thy foes." (D&C 121:7–8.)

The Book of Mormon contains a most meaningful account of Nephi, the son of Helaman. Nephi lived in a time of great wickedness. His efforts to draw the people back to the Lord had been largely futile. Nephi fell into a state of despondency. The record tells us:

And it came to pass as he was thus pondering— being much cast down because of the wickedness of the people . . . a voice came unto him saying:

Blessed art thou, Nephi, for those things which thou hast done; for I have beheld how thou hast with unwearyingness declared the word, which I have given unto thee, unto this people. And thou hast not feared them, and hast not sought thine own life, but hast sought my will, and to keep my commandments.

And now, because thou hast done this with such unwearyingness, behold, I will bless thee forever; and I will make thee mighty in word and in deed, in faith and in works; yea, even that all things shall be done unto thee according to thy word, for thou shalt not ask that which is contrary to my will.

Nephi had demonstrated that he could be entrusted with the powers of God. He had proved himself fully accountable to do the right things for the right reasons. The Lord's pronouncement to him is impressive: "Behold, thou art Nephi: and I am God. Behold, I declare it unto thee in the presence of mine angels, that ye shall have power over this people." (Helaman 10:3-5, 6.)

The same promise is given to all who will prove themselves accountable as Nephi had done.

We should live in such a way that we will one day be personally accountable before God in doing all that he expects of us—not because we are compelled to do so, but because it has become our own will as well as his.

CHAPTER THREE

Developing
Strength Within

*E*ach generation of the human family has had its particular set of challenges to face. Those of past generations who looked ahead in vision to our own day spoke of it with awesome premonition. Paul wrote to his young friend Timothy:

> This know also, that in the last days perilous times shall come.
> For men shall be lovers of their own selves, covetous, boasters, proud, blasphemers, disobedient to parents, unthankful, unholy,
> Without natural affection, trucebreakers, false accusers, incontinent, fierce, despisers of those that are good,
> Traitors, heady, highminded, lovers of pleasures more than lovers of God; . . .
> Ever learning, and never able to come to the knowledge of the truth. (2 Timothy 3:1-4, 7.)

The Old Testament prophet Joel looked upon our time and said:

"Proclaim ye this among the Gentiles; Prepare war, wake up the mighty men, let all the men of war draw near; let them come up: beat your plowshares into swords, and your pruninghooks into spears: let the weak say, I am strong" (Joel 3:9–10).

And then, as though to let us be aware that the strife to which he alluded was not of a physical nature only, Joel spoke of the struggle that would ensue for the minds of the people: "Multitudes, multitudes in the valley of decision: for the day of the Lord is near in the valley of decision" (Joel 3:14).

How can we develop the strength that Joel charges us to have? Are there any keys to acquiring the inner strength and stability we will need to survive in a world like the one Paul describes?

The more I experience of life, and the more I have opportunity to observe the lives of others, the more convinced I become that some of the key factors in this quest for strength are these:

1. Faith and confidence in a beneficent Power that has ultimate control of the universe and that intervenes in our own personal lives and circumstances.

2. A purpose in life that gives us a sense of direction for the things we do.

3. A basic code of conduct or set of guiding principles that are harmonious with our purpose in life and that steer our actions and our thoughts.

4. Consistent compliance with this code of conduct.

5. Self-worth and self-esteem that allow us to be charitable toward our own imperfections without becoming tolerant of them.

6. A regard for the worth of others and an acceptance of their need for achieving progress and happiness.

7. An ability to regenerate enthusiasm and hope, even after failures.

8. Patience that does not degenerate into apathy, and a fundamental optimism in the final outcome of things.

Let me briefly comment on each of these keys. First, the need for trust in a divine Power. For those of us who are Latter-day Saints, that Power is personified in the Godhead. Our first article of faith says, "We believe in God, the Eternal Father, and in His Son, Jesus Christ, and in the Holy Ghost."

Joseph Smith pointed out that faith or trust in Deity becomes efficacious for us when we (1) believe that God exists; (2) understand his true attributes; and (3) know that the course we are following coincides with his will.

I know of nothing that I value more than the assurance I have that there is an Eternal Father in heaven; a Savior of mankind, who is Jesus Christ; and a Holy Spirit who can inspire, comfort, and guide us. While the experiences that have brought me to this assurance are no more dramatic or impressive than those others enjoy in their own lives, they have been sufficient to convince me beyond question that we have a God who is omnipotent and who is aware of each of us. Those occurrences that bring us closest to him are very personal and sacred. Perhaps it would not be inappropriate to share here one such experience of my own that occurred early in my life at a time when I felt that I needed help beyond my own capacity and resources. It had a profound influence on my personal faith in and love for my Heavenly Father. I have never forgotten its impact upon me. In retrospect, it was not an earthshaking crisis that led to this experience, but at the time it seemed so to me. Let me give it to you as I have recorded it in my personal history. It has to do with my service in the navy while I was aboard the aircraft carrier *Saratoga*. I had enlisted as a seventeen-year-old, never in my life having been away from my home and family before.

"I have few favorable memories of my time aboard the *Saratoga*. I made very few friends, mostly because I did not extend myself to others. I was fearful of being drawn into situations which I could not control, and, therefore, avoided going on shore leave with other crew members when we were in port. I had been on board the ship for six months before I finally mustered enough courage to go ashore. This decision led me into a harrowing experience which eventually immeasurably enhanced my testimony of the power of prayer.

"We were tied up at the naval air station at Alameda, California, just south of Oakland in the San Francisco Bay. I had learned from other crew members that there was a theater at the air station which presented movies on a nightly basis. Consequently, when it came the turn of my division to draw liberty for an evening I picked up my liberty card for the first time from my division officer and went ashore late in the afternoon. I was alone. The liberty card which gave me clearance to leave the ship was a small plastic-covered card with my name, serial number, and division on it. It was much like the ID cards that servicemen always wore around their necks.

"In order to get on and off the ship for liberty, or shore leave, a crew member was required to present his liberty card to the officer of the deck, who stood at the head of the gangway leading to and from the ship. Anyone attempting to board the ship without a liberty card was immediately called into question by the officer of the deck. If the sailor in such an instance was found to be a member of the crew, he was pronounced absent without leave and was promptly locked in the stockade pending an investigation of his circumstances. At this particular time, with the war being ended and many of the old veterans impatient to be free of the service routine, there had been a radical increase in the number of men leaving the ship without permission, or failing to return from leave at the proper time. This situation had led the commanding staff of the ship to become very severe with anyone who appeared as AWOL (absent without official leave).

"Knowing of the rigidity with which leave procedures were being enforced had been one of the deterrents to my taking liberty earlier. I was afraid of having something happen while ashore that would make it impossible for me to return to the ship in proper order, thereby placing me in jeopardy of my freedom and my record of good conduct.

"On this particular occasion, however, I was certain I would have no difficulty if I simply went to the theater on the air base and then returned immediately and directly to the ship. Besides, I was anxious to get the feel of solid ground under my feet again, even if only for a few hours.

"I left the ship and walked the mile or so to the theater on the air base. The only thing necessary for admission to the theater was to show one's liberty card if he happened to be a crew member of one of the ships in the docks at the air station. I went through this process and enjoyed seeing a regular movie for the first time in many months. Following the movie, I went directly back to the ship. As I started to mount the gangway I withdrew my wallet from my pocket in order to extract my liberty card for presentation to the officer of the deck. To my absolute dismay, I could not find the card in my wallet.

"I stopped half-way up the gangway and searched through my wallet and my pockets over and over again for my card. It soon became obvious that I did not have it with me. My mind ran quickly back over the events of the evening in an effort to determine where the card might have been lost. I realized then that the only place I had taken the card from my wallet was in the theater lobby where I had had to show it in order to be admitted to the movie. Surely it must have been dropped in the theater lobby.

"I ran down the gangway and made record time back to the theater, praying with all my heart that someone would be there who had found my liberty card and held it for me.

"When I reached the theater, my heart sank. It was locked up and completely dark. No one was about. I tried all the doors—but to no avail. By this time I was close to a feeling of panic. The thought of returning to the ship without my card and of being taken to the ship's brig under arrest for being AWOL was more than I could stand. I envisioned such a report reaching my parents and family, and I knew the distress that would be caused regardless of my innocence. It was a mighty distasteful thing to contemplate.

"The thought occurred to me that the card might have somehow been kicked outside the lobby onto the cement steps that led up to the building's entrance. I covered every inch of those steps in sheer desperation, not just once but many times, hoping with a desperate hope that it would by some miracle be there. It wasn't.

"Finally, completely frustrated and frightened, I sat down on one of the steps to the building, put my head in my hands, and with the greatest sense of need for help, I asked Heavenly Father to bless me. I explained to him how concerned I was about the distress that would be caused for my family if they were to learn that I had been in jail. It would be a difficult thing to explain. I told Him I had tried everything I could think of on my own, and now I needed his help. I believe it was the first time in my life that I had prayed with a need that was urgent enough to outweigh any questions as to whether there was an efficacy in prayer. I simply needed help beyond myself, and I knew it.

"When I finished my prayer, I lifted my head and my hands fell down to my sides on the cement steps. My left hand fell directly on my liberty card. It was immediately beside me on the step, right in the place where my hand had fallen.

"I cannot describe the feeling that flooded over me with this discovery. It was a mixture of surprise, disbelief, overwhelming relief, and awe. I sat momentarily and cried in my relief. It hardly seemed possible. I *knew* the card had not been there before. It was completely unlikely that it would ever have been outside the building at all. I was stunned at this direct and, apparently, miraculous answer to my prayer.

"I returned to the ship and went directly to my bunk where I offered up another prayer—this one a prayer of thanksgiving for what will always be, to me, a miraculous response from my Father in Heaven who was listening when I needed him so much."

It is not enough to believe in the existence of Deity. That belief must be based on a true understanding of who and what he is. Jesus said, "And this is life eternal, that they might *know* thee the only true God, and Jesus Christ, whom thou hast sent" (John 17:3, italics added). To believe in God is good, but to *know* him is essential to the kind of personal strength we require. One who does not possess this knowledge is at a great disadvantage.

The second key to personal stability and strength is to have a vision of life's purpose. Purpose circumscribes existence. It provides guideposts and direction. Without purpose, life has no compass. Almost all of us know of people whose life's efforts have brought them wealth, power, and notoriety but have ended in despair and disappointment. Stephen Leacock referred to such people in his essay titled "Education Is Eating Up Life":

"How strange it is, our little process of life! The child says, 'When I am a big boy.' But what is that? The big boy says, 'When I grow up.' And then, grown up, he says, 'When I get married.' But to be married, what is that, after all? The thought changes to 'When I am able to retire.' And then, when retirement comes, he looks back over the landscape traversed; a cold wind seems to sweep over it; somehow he has missed it all, and it is gone."

Life with a purpose can be lived so that there is a sense of enduring progress and achievement. Random accomplishments and acquisitions may fail to bring the contentment and peace of mind upon which inner strength depends.

The third key I have suggested is the possession of a code of conduct or set of guiding principles that harmonizes with our life's purpose. For those of us who have membership in the Church of Jesus Christ, the gospel of Christ provides such a code. It encompasses principles that are eternal. They do not change with time or circumstances. What a tremendous advantage we have in the possession of these principles! We can always depend upon the fact that our compliance with them will bear good fruit. Only when correct principles are understood and followed are we free to exercise choice without jeopardy to our spiritual and emotional well-being.

It has become fashionable in today's world to base behavior upon a set of flexible and shifting premises. Many tell us that our own immediate wants and desires are the most reliable guide to our conduct. As an illustration of this, I cite from one of the leading educational journals of the day:

"In choosing what course of action to take in any situation, many people rely upon guiding principles, upon a code of action laid down by some group or institution. . . . Yet as I observe . . . I find that increasingly . . . individuals are able to trust their total orgasmic reaction to a new situation because they discover to an ever-increasing degree that if they are open to their experience, doing what 'feels right' proves to be a competent and trustworthy guide to behavior."

This further comment from the same source is significant also: "Another way of saying this is that the individual guides his behavior by the meanings which he discovers in the immediate feeling process which is going on within him." (*Perceiving, Behaving, Becoming,* Association for Supervision and Curriculum Development, Washington, D.C., 1962, pp. 26–27, 28.)

Oh, the unhappiness, disillusionment, and tragedy that have come into the lives of so many who have accepted this siren song as their gospel! True principles are not changed, either in their existence or in their influence upon our lives, by our failure to recognize and comply with them. They operate continually and consistently. Their positive effect upon us may be limited by the degree to which we understand and obey them, but their overall effect, whether for good or for ill, is inevitable and unrelenting.

Religion comes in for a special indictment by those who foster the philosophy of total self-actualization. We are warned by them, "In our authoritarian culture, many forces converge upon the . . . individual which have the effect of making him think less of himself. The Church is one of these forces. The concept of guilt, with its imaginary burden of sin, cannot help one think well of himself. . . . Those who have salvation to dispense hold a powerful weapon. When one is made to feel unworthy, he is crippled in some degree, because he cannot do what he otherwise might." (*Perceiving, Behaving, Becoming,* p. 12.)

All of these protestations notwithstanding, there is no inner strength and security without the acceptance of and obedience to correct principles.

I have already made comment on the fourth key in my suggested list: *consistent compliance with correct principles or an accepted code of conduct.* It is not enough to know what is true and correct. We must follow the course we know to be right. To do otherwise is devastating to our spiritual and emotional stability. All of the rationalizing and philosophizing in the world cannot prevent this inevitable result. "My strength is as the strength of ten," Tennyson had Sir Galahad say, "because my heart is pure."

The fifth requirement in my list has to do with self-worth or self-esteem. We must be able to be charitable toward our own imperfections without becoming tolerant of them.

Joseph Smith said, "When you climb up a ladder, you must begin at the bottom, and ascend step by step, until you arrive at the top; and so it is with the principles of the Gospel—you must begin with the first, and go on until you learn all the principles of exaltation. But it will be a great while after you have passed through the veil before you will have learned them. It is not all to be comprehended in this world; it will be a great work to learn our salvation and exaltation even beyond the grave." (*Teachings of the Prophet Joseph Smith,* sel. Joseph Fielding Smith, Deseret Book Co., 1938, p. 348.)

The work of perfecting ourselves is one that will continue beyond mortal life. Our principal challenge here is to bring our lives into basic harmony with the fundamental principles of progress and eternal happiness. Occasionally all of us fall short of being our very best. It is part of enduring to pick ourselves up when we have stumbled, and then move on.

One of the unfortunate circumstances of the complex, stressful pattern of life so many of us follow is that we create so many particular requirements by which to evaluate ourselves. So many diverse expectations are thus laid upon us. It is not difficult to recognize our imperfections in the midst of all these requirements and expectations. There is likely not a soul among us who is not vulnerable to these feelings at times. But if we become too critical of ourselves, we work against our best interests. Emerson said: "Finish every day and be done with it. You have done what you could. Some blunders and absurdities no doubt crept in; forget them as soon as you can. Tomorrow is a new day; begin it well and serenely and with too high a spirit to be cumbered with your old nonsense."

While we must not tolerate our imperfections to the degree that we become complacent and at ease with them, we need to recognize that we will not overcome all of them immediately. Sometimes it is helpful to focus upon one facet of our lives until we have sensed a measure of mastery, and then transfer our energies and attentions to another. We must maintain a kind of balance in this effort. Bryant S. Hinckley said: "If we are over-enthusiastic, our enthusiasms may become fanaticism. If we are strongly emotional, our emotions may lead to hysterics. If we are overly imaginative, we may become visionary and flighty. If we have a super-abundance of courage, it may manifest itself in recklessness. . . . Piety may become sanctimoniousness. And so every virtue may become a vice—every grace a defect. It is the fine balance of these virtues that makes a strong man." (*A Study of the Character and Teachings of Jesus of Nazareth,* Presiding Bishop's Office, 1952, pp. 169–70.)

Those who drive themselves unmercifully toward perfection on too broad a plane may well bring themselves to a state of mental and emotional despair.

I read an article in one of the airline magazines that seemed to have a bearing on this point. It had to do with the people whom we refer to as "workaholics." The general perception has been that such people are apt to excel and become enviable assets to the company or enterprise with which they are associated, but this seems to be changing. I quote from the article: "A new theory is creeping into American boardrooms. The man or woman who is job-obsessed could actually be a drain on the bottom line. The lust for fourteen-hour days is being recognized as more than a way to plug voids in personal lives. What passed as supreme dedication a decade ago is deemed disruptive by some companies today. What's more, the manager who flogs himself as an example to his troops may be triggering tremendous turnover, or even stress-induced workers' compensation claims by subordinates, or lawsuits."

The article also asserts that workaholics "tend to come to work in crisis oriented moods. They also tend to be undisciplined people, unable to set appropriate schedules and manage themselves." (*Republic Scene,* January 1982, pp. 39, 71.)

When we press ourselves too relentlessly and unforgivingly toward perfection, we not only run the risk of robbing our own lives of stability and self-esteem but we may also have a very negative effect upon those whose lives are most closely intertwined with our own. We must be as considerate and charitable toward our own weaknesses as we are toward those of a good friend whom we love and much admire in spite of his failings. Everyone needs to feel successful and worthy in some ways at least part of the time. The best progress sometimes occurs when we are not under intense duress. Overzealousness is at least as much to be feared as apathy.

Jacob, the brother of Nephi, quoted in the Book of Mormon an interesting allegory from the writings of the prophet Zenos. The allegory has to do with olive trees and a vineyard, and the effort required to keep these trees producing good fruit. When the trees become wild and their fruit is no longer desirable, the Lord of the vineyard undertakes an analysis with his servants to determine the cause of the deterioration. The diagnosis of one of the servants is most interesting and meaningful. "And it came to pass that the servant said unto his master: Is it not the loftiness of thy vineyard—have not the branches thereof overcome the roots . . . taking strength unto themselves. . . ." (Jacob 5:48.)

Sometimes the expectations we place upon ourselves can overreach our capacity to cope with them. We branch out into so many channels that we do not have the strength or the resources to sustain the effort. In Zenos's allegory the master of the vineyard proposes a most practical solution to the problem of the over-grown branches. "Ye shall clear away the branches which bring forth bitter fruit, according to the strength of the good and the size thereof; and ye shall not clear away the bad thereof all at once, . . . wherefore ye shall clear away the bad according as the good shall grow, that the root and the top may be equal in strength, until the good shall overcome the bad.'' (Jacob 5:65-66.)

Is there not in this allegory an excellent lesson for us respecting the manner in which we might work toward our own improvement while maintaining a sense of self-worth?

The sixth key relates to our regard for the worth of others and their need for achieving happiness.

We can never experience personal security if we are fearful of others rising above us. Real strength does not develop, nor is it properly exercised, by holding others down so that we are a focal point of attention and influence. The Savior demonstrated this fact perfectly in his own life and ministry. His whole purpose was to lift and exalt others. His position in the Godhead was not achieved, nor is it maintained, by suppression. He is not threatened by the achievements and progress of others. He glories in it. His strength derives from a disposition to elevate others. Truly strong individuals need not dominate others. They are secure in their motivation to lift and bless. Somehow they seem to be magnified by the reflections that are directed back to them in the accomplishments of those whom they may have assisted. Is not this principle manifest in the declaration of the Lord: ''For behold, this is my work and my glory—to bring to pass the immortality and eternal life of man''? (Moses 1:39.)

There is great personal peace and satisfaction in being the means of lifting and magnifying someone other than ourselves. An old Hindu proverb says, ''Help thy brother's boat across—and lo, thine own has reached the shore.''

Joseph F. Smith said: ''Look for good in men, and where they fail to possess it, try to build it up in them;

48

try to increase the good in them; look for the good; build up the good; sustain the good; and speak as little about the evil as you possibly can" (*Gospel Doctrine*, Deseret Book Co., 1966, p. 254).

I have suggested as the seventh key for personal strength the capacity to regenerate enthusiasm and hope, even after failures.

We are told in the scriptures that those who endure to the end will be saved (see 2 Nephi 31:15). I have thought that *enduring*, as it is mentioned in the scriptures, reflects as much an attitude of mind as it does the accomplishment or completion of a particular phase of our existence. One who has an *enduring* attitude is not easily discouraged or defeated. Personal freedom, accountability, and initiative are prized by those who understand the principle of enduring. They do not look quickly for crutches to depend upon. They do not readily pass the responsibility for their own failures to others. They discover sources both within themselves and outside themselves for renewal and redirection. Personally, I know of no better source for this kind of help than that which comes through earnest prayer and through studying and pondering the scriptures. I have learned that confiding problems and setbacks too quickly and too freely to friends or relatives may actually result in complicating matters and making solutions more difficult. This kind of result never occurs when we resort to prayer. Of course, there are appropriate times to seek the counsel and support of trusted friends and loved ones, but I have learned that it is often as wise to keep personal matters confidential as it is to preserve the confidences that are entrusted to us by others.

Finally, I believe inner strength requires that we possess great patience. It is interesting to see how frequently the writers of the scriptures speak of patience and faith as essential companions. Things of great worth often mature slowly. I am much impressed by the analogy that Alma uses in his great discourses on the development of faith. He likens the nourishing of faith to the nourishment of a tree as it grows. It is significant that Alma did not select the dandelion or the alfalfa plant for his analogy. He chose the tree because of its slow growth.

"But if ye neglect the tree," Alma said, "and take no thought for its nourishment, behold it will not get any root; and when the heat of the sun cometh and scorcheth it, because it hath no root it withers away, and ye pluck it up and cast it out." And he added: "But if ye will . . . nourish the tree as it beginneth to grow, by your faith with great diligence, and with patience, looking forward to the fruit thereof, it shall take root; and behold it shall be a tree springing up unto everlasting life." (Alma 32:41.)

Patience must be one of the prominent attributes of the Lord. Perhaps his capacity to exercise patience comes from the fact that he knows the end from the beginning and he has a basis for trusting in the final outcome of things. He knows he will prevail. If we can draw upon that same source of strength, our lives will be more secure. Patience requires trust. Trust is closely related to faith. When we know also that the Lord's work and his justice and mercy will ultimately prevail, we can gain peace of mind and consolation, even when things do not go as well as we had hoped or planned; and especially when they do not comply with our personal timetable.

In all of our concern about developing an inner, sustaining strength, we cannot forget the principal purpose for our coming into mortal life. That purpose is to give us experience in an environment where we can be tested and proved. Carlyle said, "The brightest crowns that are worn in heaven have been tried and smelted and polished and glorified through the furnace of tribulation." (Quoted at Women's Conference at Brigham Young University on February 19, 1982.)

CHAPTER FOUR

Accountability as a Member of the House of Israel

So much of scriptural history is directly related to the people who bear the name of Israel. From the information the Lord has revealed, some of the most dramatic events to take place upon the earth are yet to occur, and Israel will play the principal role in many of these events. An understanding of Israel is essential for Latter-day Saints. Who they were, who they are, what the Lord expects of them, our relationship to this covenant people—all of these things are of great importance.

It is well for us to understand how the present-day efforts of the Church—its growth and expansion—relate to the promises made by the Lord to Israel. As we contemplate the predicted gathering and restoration of Israel, we can learn much about what our own future may be—the conditions and events through which we may yet pass, and the role the Lord expects us to play. We also gain an increased appreciation for the determination of the Lord to fulfill every promise he has made to those who are a part of the chosen, covenant people.

In order to understand the Lord's purpose in establishing a people with a special mission and purpose, it is necessary to go back to the time of Abraham. Abraham "sought for the blessings of the fathers, and the right whereunto I shall be ordained to administer the same" (Abraham 1:2). In response to Abraham's appeal, the Lord made a covenant with him. This covenant not only reflects the blessings for which Abraham and his posterity might qualify; it specifies the obligations for service and sacrifice that they would incur. "I will make of thee a great nation," the Lord said to Abraham, "and I will bless thee above measure, and make thy name great among all nations, and thou shalt be a blessing unto thy seed after thee, that in their hands they shall bear this ministry and Priesthood unto all nations" (Abraham 2:9).

It is clear that in making his covenant with Abraham the Lord intended to establish a people who could serve as his agents in taking the opportunities for salvation and exaltation to all the people of the earth. There would be great privileges and blessings associated with this special designation, but there would also be sobering burdens of responsibility imposed. The Lord's love and concern for his covenant people is no greater than that he feels for the rest of his children. It is important to understand this "agent" role placed by the Lord upon Abraham and his posterity. An association with the house of Israel carries with it an accountability for contributing to the fulfillment of the Lord's purposes among all his children.

In his book *The Covenant People*, W. J. Cameron describes well what it means to carry this special responsibility. He writes:

A man will rise and demand, "By what right does God choose one race of people above another?" I like that form of the question. It is much better than asking by what right God degrades one people beneath another, although that is implied. God's grading is always upward. If He raises up a nation, it is that other nations may be raised up through its ministry. If He exalts a great man, an apostle of liberty, or science, or faith, it is that He might raise a degraded people to a better condition. The Divine selection is not a prize, a compliment paid to the man or the race—it is a burden imposed. To appoint a chosen people is not a pandering to the racial vanity of a "superior people"; it is a yoke bound upon the necks of those who are chosen for a special service. (*The Covenant People*, Destiny Publishers, Merrimac, Massachusetts, 1966, p. 8.)

In his blessing to Abraham, the Lord indicated that through the priesthood that would be confirmed upon Abraham and his posterity, and through his literal descendants "shall all the families of the earth be blessed, even with the blessings of the Gospel, which are the blessings of salvation, even of life eternal" (Abraham 2:11). "And I will bless them through thy name," the Lord said, "for as many as receive this Gospel shall be called after thy name, and shall be accounted thy seed, and shall rise up and bless thee as their father" (Abraham 2:10).

So in the covenant he made with Abraham the Lord provided a way to extend the possibilities of salvation and exaltation to all of his children. This covenant was renewed with Isaac, Abraham's son (see Genesis 17:19–21), and later with Jacob, to whom the Lord said: "I am the Lord God of Abraham thy father, and the God of Isaac. . . . And thy seed shall be as the dust of the earth, and thou shalt spread abroad to the west, and to the east, and to the north, and to the south: and in thee and in thy seed shall all the families of the earth be blessed." (Genesis 28:13–14.)

At a later time the Lord told Jacob, "Thy name shall not be called any more Jacob, but Israel shall be thy name: and he called his name Israel" (Genesis 35:10). So in Jacob's generation the name *Israel* was applied to the people of the covenant. The sons of Jacob became the heads of separate tribes—the tribes of Israel.

Anyone familiar with the Old Testament record will know of the fascinating story regarding how the family of Jacob found their way into Egypt during a time of famine, when Joseph, one of the sons, had become the governor of that land under Pharaoh. For more than four hundred years they remained in Egypt, during which time they grew into a great nation of people and suffered much hardship.

Following their miraculous escape from Egypt under the leadership of Moses, the people of Israel returned to the lands that had been promised to their fathers as part of the Lord's covenant. In this transition they demonstrated what a difficult, fractious, rebellious people they could be. The Lord and his appointed leaders experienced many disappointments as they attempted to establish among Israel faith and obedience sufficient to qualify them for the "agent" role conferred upon them by the Lord in earlier times.

For a time, back in their land of promise, Israel showed some prospect of rising to the task the Lord had assigned to them, thereby qualifying for the special blessings promised through their fathers. Sections of the land were designated for each of the family tribes, with

Joseph's two sons, Manasseh and Ephraim, receiving inheritances in full stature with the families of the other sons of Jacob. Notable leaders, such as Joshua, David, and Solomon established the nation of Israel as a leading power, commanding the attention and often the obeisance of the great figures of the area.

But power, wealth, and ease brought eventual corruption. Spiritual degeneracy was followed by political strife and divisiveness. Shortly before 900 B.C. the house of Israel separated into two kingdoms. Ten of the tribes formed a northern kingdom with a center of government in Samaria. They were known as Israel, or the northern kingdom. Some histories refer to this kingdom as Ephraim, since the people of Ephraim became dominant among its leaders.

The southern kingdom included the tribe of Judah along with much of the tribe of Benjamin and fragments of other tribes who identified nationally with the southern group. Jerusalem remained the capital of this kingdom, which took the name of Judah.

Thus the house of Israel became divided. The southern kingdom remained somewhat more faithful to the worship of Jehovah for a time, but apostasy soon overcame both groups. The decline in spiritual strength was accompanied by a decline in political power and influence.

After a history of two hundred years, the northern kingdom was conquered by an Assyrian army and most of the people were carried away captive into Assyria. The warnings of the prophets had gone unheeded. The predicted calamities had come. The ten northern tribes were lost.

Judah soon followed the course of their northern counterparts. Apostasy and corruption inevitably prevailed. About 135 years after the conquest of Israel by the Assyrians, Judah was overrun by the Babylonian empire under King Nebuchadnezzar. Many of the Jews were carried away as captives into Babylon.

Isaiah and Jeremiah, who witnessed the decline of the house of Israel, lamented the terrible destruction which they envisioned for their people. They predicted a long period of chastening under the Lord's hand. ". . . this is a rebellious people," said Isaiah, "lying children, children that will not hear the law of the Lord: which say to the seers, See not; and to the prophets, Prophesy not unto us right things, speak unto us smooth things, prophesy deceits" (Isaiah 30:9–10). He speaks of a prolonged period during which Israel will be "barren," "forsaken," and "desolate" (see Isaiah 54:1).

Jeremiah described his people in this way: "And they bend their tongues like their bow for lies: but they are not valiant for the truth upon the earth; for they proceed from evil to evil, and they know not me, saith the Lord." Through Jeremiah too the Lord promised, "I will scatter them also among the heathen, whom neither they nor their fathers have known: and I will send a sword after them, till I have consumed them." (Jeremiah 9:3, 16.)

In this brief historical synopsis we have a glimpse of the house of Israel in early times. Israel's ancient identity was confined in large measure to the literal descendants of Abraham, Isaac, and Jacob. Their influence was geographically limited to those lands inhabited by the early kingdoms of Israel and Judah. But it was not always to be so.

Abraham had been told by the Lord that in some way, through the literal seed of his body, all the families of the earth would be blessed (see Abraham 2:11). This obviously does not imply that everyone on the earth would be of the literal seed of Abraham, but it does seem to suggest that the day would come when those who are descendants of the original covenant people would be found scattered among the nations. As we have seen, to Jacob the Lord had said that his seed would "spread abroad to the west, and to the east, and to the north, and to the south" (Genesis 28:14).

In view of these promises, and in light of the historical captivity and scattering of the tribes of Israel, the questions might well be asked: "Where is Israel today? Who are those of the house of Israel in our own time?"

A careful review of the scriptures will help us to find at least partial answers to these questions. It may also help us to see the present-day work of the Church in a new and more interesting perspective, and to understand more fully some of the significant events that are still ahead of us as the Lord fulfills his covenant with Israel and holds them accountable for providing eternal opportunities for all his children.

Let us look, first of all, at the house of Israel today. At least two segments of Israel have retained some degree of their racial identity over the centuries. The Jews are one of these. While there was obviously some mixing in the earlier period when Benjamin and fragments of other tribes joined in the southern kingdom, and while some mixing has certainly occurred in the intervening years, the tribe of Judah has preserved an identity to our present day. Their dispersion worldwide has not obscured this identity.

One other group that can be recognized racially to some degree are those who came to the Americas at the time of the Babylonian conquest of Judah. These are the people of the Book of Mormon. We have been inclined to refer to them generally today as Lamanites. They are spoken of in the Book of Mormon in general terms as a remnant of Joseph. We know, however, that among this group there was considerable mixing. Lehi and his party were Josephites. Those who came with Mulek, the son of King Zedekiah, were apparently of Judah, which may account in part for the Lord's referring to Book of Mormon peoples today as remnants of the Jews. (D&C 19:27.) While much mixing has occurred in more recent times with the "gentile" nations that have come to the Americas, there is still a racial identity among millions of these people throughout North and South America, Central America, and some islands of the Pacific.

A third segment of Israel continuing to the present day are those spoken of as the lost tribes. Their location is unknown at present. That at least part of them have remained together in a somewhat coherent group is indicated in several of the scriptures. Nephi spoke of the records which the lost tribes would keep and which one day would be available as a separate scripture (see 2 Nephi 29:12–14).

The Savior, at the time of his visit to the Americas, announced that he had been commanded by the Father to go to these tribes and manifest himself to them so that they would have a witness and a record of his resurrection. (3 Nephi 16:1–3; 17:4.)

He also referred to a time when they will apparently have the gospel preached to them in the last days, preparatory to their return. (3 Nephi 21:1–7, 26.)

The Lord revealed to Joseph Smith that the day would come when "they who are in the north countries shall come in remembrance before the Lord; and their prophets shall hear his voice, and shall no longer stay themselves; and they shall smite the rocks, and the ice shall flow down at their presence. And an highway shall be cast up in the midst of the great deep." (D&C 133:26–27.)

This seems to confirm Jeremiah's prediction: "In those days the house of Judah shall walk with the house of Israel, and they shall come together out of the land of the north to the land that I have given for an inheritance unto your fathers" (Jeremiah 3:18).

Joseph Smith predicted a time of destruction and turmoil in the United States in preparation "for the return of the lost tribes of Israel from the north country." (*Teachings of the Prophet Joseph Smith*, p. 17.)

A fourth segment of the house of Israel is represented by those who would be scattered among all the nations of the earth and who would, in some measure at least, become identified with the Gentiles. Of this group Nephi wrote:

". . . for it appears that the house of Israel, sooner or later, will be scattered upon all the face of the earth, and also among all nations. . . . Wherefore, they shall be scattered among all nations and shall be hated of all men." (1 Nephi 22:3, 5.)

It appears that among this group would be many of the tribe of Ephraim, who would be sought out in the final restoration to lay the foundation for the latter-day work of establishing the Church and kingdom of God upon the earth.

It is significant that Joseph Smith, in his revealed dedicatory prayer for the Kirtland Temple, said: "Now these words, O Lord, we have spoken before thee, concerning the revelations and commandments which thou hast given unto us, who are identified with the Gentiles" (D&C 109:60).

Speaking of those in the north countries who shall return in the last days, the Lord referred to their coming to the children of Ephraim, among whom the gospel would be had, in order to receive their blessings (see D&C 133:32).

A fifth group who must be identified with Israel in this present day are those from among the truly gentile peoples who accept the gospel, repent of their sins, are baptized, and receive the ordinances and covenants that pertain to eternal life. Of these, the Lord said to Abraham: "And I will bless them through thy name; for as many as receive this Gospel shall be called after thy name, and shall be accounted thy seed, and shall rise up and bless thee, as their father" (Abraham 2:10).

Nephi wrote: "For behold, I say unto you that as many of the Gentiles as will repent are the covenant people of the Lord" (2 Nephi 30:2). The angel confirmed this with Nephi when he said, in reference to the Latter-day restoration: "And it shall come to pass, that if the Gentiles shall hearken unto the Lamb of God in that day that he shall manifest himself unto them in word, and also in power, in very deed, unto the taking away of their stumbling blocks—and harden not their hearts against the Lamb of God, they shall be numbered among the seed of thy father; yea, *they shall be numbered among the house of Israel*; and they shall be a blessed people upon the promised land forever" (1 Nephi 14:1-2, italics added).

And the Savior himself said: "If the Gentiles will repent and return unto me, saith the Father, behold, they shall be numbered among my people, O house of Israel" (3 Nephi 16:13).

The above is a cursory look at the house of Israel in the last days as revealed in the scriptures.

Jeremiah, Isaiah, and others who wrote and prophesied of Israel's ancient misfortunes also had much to say about the time in which we live, when the Lord would again establish Israel in its prophetic role. Jeremiah said: "Therefore, behold, the days come, saith the Lord, that it shall no more be said, The Lord liveth, that brought up the children of Israel out of the land of Egypt; but, the Lord liveth, that brought up the children of Israel from the land of the north, and from all the lands whither he had driven them: and I will bring them again into their land that I gave unto their fathers. Behold, I will send for many fishers, saith the Lord, and they shall fish them; and after will I send for many hunters, and they shall hunt them from every mountain, and from every hill, and out of the holes of the rocks." (Jeremiah 16:14–16.)

The fishing and the hunting are progressing at an increasing rate; and it is extending to a broader and broader base.

Isaiah wrote of the day of Israel's restoration in these terms:

"Sing, O barren, thou that didst not bear; break forth into singing, and cry aloud, thou that didst not travail with child. . . . Enlarge the place of thy tent, and let them stretch forth the curtains of thine habitations: spare not, lengthen thy cords, and strengthen thy stakes; for thou shalt break forth on the right hand and on the left; and thy seed shall inherit the Gentiles, and make the desolate cities to be inhabited. . . . And all thy children shall be taught of the Lord; and great shall be the peace of thy children." (Isaiah 54:1–3, 13.)

The tenth article of faith refers specifically to the restoration of the ten tribes. Some reference to them has already been made. There has been much speculation about who they are and where they are. Many of these questions do not have present answers. In his instructions to the people of Nephi during his brief ministry among them, the Savior gave some insights that are interesting to contemplate. He had much to say about the latter-day gathering of Israel and their relationship to those who are called Gentiles. In 3 Nephi these words of the Savior are recorded:

> And verily I say unto you, I give unto you a sign, that ye may know the time when these things shall be about to take place—that I shall gather in, from their long dispersion, my people, O house of Israel, and shall establish again among them my Zion;
>
> And behold, this is the thing which I will give unto you for a sign. . . .
>
> When these things come to pass that thy seed shall begin to know these things—it shall be a sign unto them, that they may know that the work of the Father hath already commenced unto the fulfilling of the covenant which he hath made unto the people who are of the house of Israel. . . .
>
> And then shall the work of the Father commence at that day, even when this gospel shall be preached among the remnant of this people. Verily I say unto you, at that day shall the work of the Father commence among all the dispersed of my people, yea, even the tribes which hath been lost. (3 Nephi 21:1-2, 7, 26.)

The terms "thy seed" and "the remnant of this people" in the context of these verses obviously refer to the people we call Lamanites today. They are the seed or the remnant of those to whom the Savior spoke these words. When we consider that there are as many stakes of the Church organized among these people today as there were in the entire Church during the administration of President David O. McKay, it appears we can safely consider that the sign spoken of has been given.

It is well for us to consider our lives, our service, our part in the Lord's work, within the perspective of these historical developments. We live in a most significant time. The events of our day are part of a divine plan. They are prophetic. It is a day of fulfillment—a day of destiny for the house of Israel.

As we look back over this long history, and as we attempt to gain some view of what is ahead, perhaps one or two additional things are worthy of particular note.

While the promises to Israel are sure, their fulfillment in individual lives is dependent upon obedience. God's dealings with his covenant people have confirmed this. His expectations for Israel are high. If we are ever inclined to claim some special status or privilege simply because we belong to this people, we may well remember the days of Jeremiah and Isaiah. And we should recall the Savior's response to the Jews who made such unmerited claims: "Think not to say within yourselves, we have Abraham to our father: for I say unto you, that God is able of these stones to raise up children unto Abraham" (Matthew 3:9).

Ours is a great privilege, but it is also a burden fastened upon our necks. Our obligations are great. As Abraham's seed, it is in our hands to "bear this ministry and Priesthood unto all nations" (Abraham 2:9).

May we be worthy of this trust and thereby qualify for an eternal inheritance with those who have been found worthy to be of Israel, the Lord's covenant people.

CHAPTER FIVE

Accountability as a Light to Others

*T*he Lord has made it clear that each of us has a responsibility to exert an influence for good in the lives of those who share this mortal experience with us. We cannot live in isolation from others and still fulfill the purpose of our existence. Our actions, our words, our thoughts, and our values will inevitably affect the souls of those whose lives brush against ours. In fact, the Lord himself said that this influence may continue to reverberate long after we have departed, even to the ensuing generations (see Mosiah 13:13). This is an awesome prospect. When we contemplate the power we have for affecting the lives of others for both good and evil, we have good reason to reach for careful understanding of this power.

It is clear that we will be held responsible for making our influence felt. There is no safety or sanctuary in living passively or in avoiding contact with others. This is true for individuals as well as groups. Nowhere in scripture is this made more emphatic than in the Lord's injunction to Ezekiel:

> Son of man, I have made thee a watchman unto the house of Israel; therefore hear the word at my mouth, and give them warning from me.
>
> When I say unto the wicked, Thou shalt surely die; and thou givest him not warning, nor speakest to warn the wicked from his wicked way, to save his life; the same wicked man shall die in his iniquity; but his blood will I require at thine hand.
>
> Yet if thou warn the wicked, and he turn not from his wickedness, nor from his wicked way, he shall die in his iniquity; but thou hast delivered thy soul. (Ezekiel 3:17–19.)

In his discourse to the Nephites the Savior said: "I give unto you to be the salt of the earth; but if the salt shall lose its savor wherewith shall the earth be salted? The salt shall be thenceforth good for nothing, but to be cast out and to be trodden under foot of men." In the same sermon he spoke of the need of our placing our light on a candlestick, not under a bushel, so that it could give light to the whole house. (3 Nephi 12:13, 14–16.)

How do we exert an influence upon others so that both their lives and ours are enriched and blessed? Joseph Smith warned of the natural propensity to use such influence in an unrighteous way. He wrote: "We have learned by sad experience that it is the nature and disposition of almost all men, as soon as they get a little authority, as they suppose, they will immediately begin to exercise unrighteous dominion. Hence many are called, but few are chosen.'' (D&C 121:39–40.) Is it possible for us to have the best of motives and intentions and still produce undesirable results? In what ways can we unrighteously dominate the lives of others? Obviously this is a matter of overriding importance, for not only do we bring others into jeopardy by our misuse of this power but it appears also that our own prospects for eternal advancement are closely related to our learning to use it righteously.

In order for us to interact with each other in a correct way, it is necessary to comprehend the immense importance of the gift of agency—freedom to exercise one's own will. Of course, agency is of little productive value unless it is accompanied by knowledge and understanding. When knowledge and understanding are combined with agency, a condition is achieved that we call accountability.

Achieving accountability and helping others to achieve it are among the most important concerns of mortal life. Parents have this great responsibility with regard to their children. The Lord has said that those parents who fail in this are guilty of a serious transgression (see D&C 68:25, 27–28). Progress and development toward a celestial standard of life cannot be achieved in the absence of individual accountability. It is a process that continues after baptism.

It is helpful to review the Pearl of Great Price account, given to us by Moses, of the propositions that were advanced and the decisions made in the great council of spirits prior to the creation and habitation of this earth. In that council the purposes and opportunities of mortal life and the essential nature of agency were explained. The preeminently important role of a redeemer and atoner in this great plan was also outlined. One whom we know as Jehovah, the firstborn of the Father in the spirit, was chosen to fill this role. He was fully qualified for such an assignment. It would require attributes of unexcelled devotion, love, and perfection. Jehovah accepted the conditions of the plan and willingly agreed to comply with them. Additionally, he insisted that the honor and glory resulting from the success of this plan would remain with the Father. (See Moses 4:1–4.)

Paramount among the conditions that Jehovah espoused was that of agency—the freedom of each individual spirit to make choices and abide by the consequences of those choices. All of us who participated in that council understood well that while our decision to come into mortal life would enable us to be "added upon," the prospect of having "glory added upon [our] heads forever and ever" (Abraham 3:26) would be conditioned upon our willing obedience to those principles and practices that would make this possible. We understood that because we would be free to make choices—to exercise our agency—some would fall short of their highest potential in consequence of their disobedience. It must have been a most sobering and compelling moment in our lives. The magnitude of the step to be taken into mortal life must have seemed overwhelming to us—and indeed it was!

At this momentous time of decision-making, another prominent figure contested the plan of the Father and opposed the choice of Jehovah as the Redeemer. Taking advantage of the anxiety and doubt that must have been felt by many of the spirits in that council, he used his influence to incite a rebellion. He proposed that he should replace Jehovah as the central figure in the plan of salvation. His proposal would deny the freedom of choice to those who followed him. They would be compelled to obedience. His promise to them was that not one soul of them would be lost. Furthermore, all the honor and glory were to rest upon him. The words of the Father describe these events and their consequences for Lucifer and those who rebelled with him:

> Wherefore, because that Satan rebelled against me, and sought to destroy the agency of man, which I, the Lord God, had given him, and also, that I should give unto him mine own power; by the power of mine Only Begotten, I caused that he should be cast down;
>
> And he became Satan, yea, even the devil, the father of all lies, to deceive and to blind men, and to lead them captive at his will, even as many as would not hearken unto my voice (Moses 4:3–4).

Lucifer knew that the promise of salvation extended on his conditions was a lie. He could not have delivered the results he promised. He had two despicable motives in taking the course he did. One was to make himself an absolute dictator, having all power and glory. The other was to enslave his followers by taking from them forever their right to make choices. Obviously under such conditions all opportunity for individual progress and development would have been lost. Lucifer sought to aggrandize himself at the eternal expense of all who would submit to this proposition.

From the scriptural account of these dramatic events we gain considerable insight into the importance of Joseph Smith's inspired observation about unrighteous dominion. No person can be compelled to progress. When compulsion is used, the benefits are lost. It is an irrevocable law. Manipulation, regimentation, coercion

—for whatever motive or reason it is done—will ultimately fail to produce good results. Joseph Smith specifically warned against such things as pride, vain ambition, control, unrighteous dominion, compulsion, hypocrisy, and guile. He declared that methods of exerting influence based upon these things would cause the Spirit of the Lord to grieve, the heavens to withdraw their sanction, and, finally, the power for accomplishing good to be terminated. (See D&C 121:36-37.)

The Prophet went on to say that no power or influence can be maintained, nor should it be attempted, even within the purview of a priesthood calling, except "by persuasion, by long-suffering, by gentleness and meekness, and by love unfeigned; by kindness, and pure knowledge, which shall greatly enlarge the soul without hypocrisy, and without guile" (D&C 121:41-42).

In order for progress and development to occur, then, a person must have the freedom to exercise his own will, and he must have a knowledge of truth sufficient to make him accountable—enough to "greatly enlarge the soul." Moreover, he must have come to value the truths he has learned for himself, by his own volition, not through compulsion or intimidation from another. Under these conditions he is capable of exercising moral judgment. And he is capable of progress.

It should be pointed out that the Lord's plan does not ignore the need for occasional correction and discipline. He does not withhold the consequences of bad choices. When we err, we feel the pain. Those in positions of influence and leadership, including parents, are required to see that purity of conduct and belief is maintained among the membership of the Church. Persistent or recurring violation of the Lord's standard requires disciplinary action. His commitment to agency does not include a tolerance of sin. It is important for us to remember the fact taught by Alma to his son Corianton: Mercy cannot rob justice (see Alma 42:24–25).

While God's love for us does not diminish, he does not rescue us from the hard lessons that we must sometimes learn. Freedom always has jeopardy as its companion. Only inspired wisdom and an unrelenting commitment to truth and righteous conduct guarantee a forward course on the path of progress.

The freedom to choose our own course of action does not provide freedom from the consequences of our choices.

With these facts before us, we may consider how we are to govern ourselves in wielding the influence the Lord expects us to have upon others. These principles can apply in our relationships with family, friends, associates, and with all whom we encounter in life's journey.

Just as the ends do not always justify the means, neither do the motives always justify the methods. Lucifer sought to aggrandize himself by enslaving others. His motive for compelling others was to exalt himself above them. One may have the purest of motives for regimenting, compelling, or controlling the lives of others, but his motives will not prevent negative results from occurring in the lives of those whom his incorrect methods touch.

We have a perfect model to follow in the Savior himself. He had great power that he could have used to compel people to follow him and to be obedient to his word. Occasionally he demonstrated this power in miraculous ways, but never with the intent to command a following. It was not uncommon for him to ask that those who had been the recipients of his marvelous power keep the

matter to themselves, tell no one of it. Such was the case
with the leper Jesus healed. "See thou tell no man"
(Matthew 8:4) was the Savior's charge in this case. It was
almost as though he feared that men would follow him
because of his power rather than as a result of having
learned his truths and having valued them because they
were true.

In no incident in the mortal ministry of the Lord is
this concern made more manifest than in the case of the
multitude he fed with the loaves and fishes (see John 6).
This great gathering of people had brought no prov-
ender with them. Out of compassion for their physical
hunger, he miraculously provided food for five thousand. Their reaction to this demonstration of power was
to attempt to convince him to become their king. The
benefits of yielding subservience to one who could care
for their needs so easily were obvious. Their intentions
alarmed the Savior. He left the crowd immediately, and
during the night crossed over to the other side of the Sea
of Galilee near Capernaum. Word soon came to them of
the Lord's whereabouts, and the throng pursued him.
When they found him, they said, "Rabbi, when camest
thou hither?" (John 6:25.)

Perceiving the real purpose of their interest in him,
the Lord accused them: "Ye seek me, not because ye
saw the miracles, but because ye did eat of the loaves,
and were filled. Labour not for the meat which perisheth, but for that meat which endureth unto everlasting
life." (John 6:26–27.) The crowd then demanded another
miracle, protesting that they were not so different from
the children of Israel, for whom Moses had provided
manna in the desert.

Obviously the truths that Jesus had taught these
people had not penetrated their hearts and their under-

standing. They were untouched by the influence he had wished to effect. "I am the bread of life," he said; "he that cometh to me shall never hunger; and he that believeth on me shall never thirst." And further: "This is the bread which cometh down from heaven, that a man may eat thereof, and not die. I am the living bread which came down from heaven; if any man eat of this bread, he shall live for ever: and the bread that I will give is my flesh, which I will give for the life of the world." (John 6:35, 50–51.)

Completely untouched by understanding, the multitude was revulsed by this allegorical attempt of the Savior, and "from that time many of his disciples went back, and walked no more with him" (John 6:66).

It would not have been difficult for Jesus to continue to command the following of these people. Their welfare and their salvation meant more to him than his own life. A few more public miracles could have held them and augmented their numbers. It would have been an easy thing to do. But the essential parts of the equation were not coming together. He did not wish a following on that basis. It must have been a terribly disappointing, frustrating experience for the Master. If they would not follow him because they believed and valued the truths he taught them, he would not have them follow him at all.

From a careful review of the Lord's own methods in teaching and influencing others, it appears that he has always been greatly concerned about helping people to become accountable. His teaching is designed to give both knowledge and understanding. He has set a perfect example. And he has always honored the agency of men. When it has been necessary for him to reprove and correct, he has done so openly and directly, but always with the intent to help and to lift — never to bring honor or attention to himself, nor to bring lock-step, blind obedience to his will. The Lord does not exercise unrighteous dominion.

Following this pattern, it would seem that we must use every opportunity that comes to us to share with others the truths we have about life and its purpose. The Lord's charge to Ezekiel that we referred to at the beginning of this chapter is evidence of this. Additionally, we must continue to encourage and guide and assist in patience and in meekness, not to serve our own needs or objectives but with an eye single to the glory of the Lord and the blessing of his children.

These matters are at the very center of the gospel of Jesus Christ and the Father's plan of life for us. There is no other plan capable of producing the character and strength and independent goodness that qualifies one for eternal life. The gospel principles and the institutions of the Church provide the essential road map for us to follow, but the detail of the daily itinerary is left up to us.

The Savior trusts us to succeed because he knows of the divine spark within us. And he trusts the plan because he knows of its perfection. Even as he had to be trusted by the Father to drink of the bitter cup in those last hours of Gethsemane—those hours when he wondered and hoped momentarily that there might be an easier way—he must trust us. Even as he had to trust Peter and the other Apostles to pass the tests of the refiner's fire after he had been taken from their midst, he must trust us. There is no other way.

When we contrast the two Peters—the vacillating Peter on the night of the Savior's betrayal and humiliation before Pilate, and the calmly unshakable Apostle who later stood before the Jewish council and at the peril of his life witnessed to the divine messiahship of the Master—we too can know that the plan is valid. It is true; it is perfect.

In order for it to work its miracle for us we must go beyond that which is prescribed for us. We must do many good things of our own free will, for the power is in us wherein we are agents unto ourselves (see D&C 58:26–28).

The challenges through which we must pass in making the necessary preparations for the Lord's return will require that we develop the tempered integrity of Peter and Paul and Joseph Smith. It is an integrity to truth that cannot be imposed upon us. It is a strength that must be born and nurtured within one's own soul. It is the power of God unto salvation through Jesus Christ. We may teach, and encourage, and love, and correct one another to achieve it, but we cannot compel.

As a high school basketball coach I learned the value of what we used to call our "freelance" offense. There were times when all the practiced patterns and set plays didn't produce the desired results. At these times the freelance offense was often effective. It simply consisted of having each player take advantage of every opportunity that arose, with a minimum of form and system. It required a considerable command of the fundamentals and a keen sensitivity to the situation.

In order for people to keep the Sabbath day holy, must they have a full day of required activities prescribed for them at our chapels, or can they enjoy the necessary group worship experiences, including partaking of the sacrament, and then be trusted to govern their own conduct and find their own means of spiritual uplift on this sacred day? Can we live with the risk that some will misuse their time and opportunity? Can agency be honored in such an important matter as this?

Can parents be entrusted to teach the gospel to their children? If they fail, whose is the accountability?

In our consideration of these vital and very real issues, we must never tune out the warning sounded for us by the Prophet Joseph Smith. "It is the nature and disposition of almost all men . . . to exercise unrighteous dominion." We must remember the terrible price that has been paid in order that our agency and accountability might be preserved and enhanced. Finally, we cannot lose from our minds the picture of the Savior's heartache and disappointment as the multitude at Capernaum turned away "and walked no more with him." Another miracle could likely have held them on—another meal of the loaves and fishes. They were so precious to him. One can sense the heart-wrenching disappointment of the Savior as he turned to his Apostles and said, "Will ye also go away?" (John 6:67.)

Peter's response has meaning for all of us: "Lord, to whom shall we go? thou hast the words of eternal life" (John 6:68).

The words of eternal life, while full of transcendent hope and promise, are not easy. The pathway of progress marked by the Lord is filled with challenges and risks. But it is the only way to celestial life. As we move along that path, we have the reassurance of knowing that we follow in the footsteps of one who knows the way, who understands, and who trusts us to press on—always with his encouragement and supporting strength, but by our own effort and will. He has removed from this path every obstacle that we could not remove ourselves. He now beckons, "Come to me."

On our onward journey may we draw proper strength and help from each other, and may we be so wise as to avoid any act or desire that would unnecessarily hedge up the way for another.

CHAPTER SIX

---

*The Strength of
the Kingdom Within*

On one occasion a group of Pharisees confronted the Savior and demanded to know when the kingdom of God would come upon the earth. Their tradition had taught them that God's kingdom would be impressive in its demonstration of power and in its earthly dominion. Their question, therefore, was a challenge to the Lord's assertion that when the kingdom of God was established on the earth, it would not be like other earthly kingdoms (see John 18:36).

The Master's response on this occasion teaches a significant lesson regarding the real source of power and influence within his kingdom. He answered: "The kingdom of God cometh not with observation: neither shall they say, Lo here! or, lo there! for, behold, the kingdom of God is within you" (Luke 17:20–21).

The Savior attempted to impress his questioners with the fact that the real power in the kingdom of God is not represented in outwardly observable things. Its strength is in the quality of the lives of its members. It is in the depth of their purity, their charity, their faith, their integrity, and their devotion to truth. This great lesson escaped the perception of the Pharisees. It has significance for us today.

Today our chapels and congregations dot almost every land in the free world. Our temples will soon be within easy traveling distance of almost every member. The percentage of members who attend meetings and activities is impressive. These are encouraging signs. We hope that they are indicators of inward strength. We rejoice in the growth that has marked the development of the Church in this century, and particularly in the last decade or two. We take encouragement from our missionary successes, as rightly we should. But in all of this outward manifestation of increasing strength, we cannot forget the Savior's injunction to those who looked for the kingdom of God to manifest itself in ways that would be impressive by earthly standards. "Behold," he said, "the kingdom of God is within you."

I once attended a conference in a stake that had compiled an impressive statistical record. By all observable standards, this was a stake composed of devoted, faithful Latter-day Saints. As I met with the stake president, I was not surprised that he was anxious to review with me the excellent statistical record his people were making. The reports had been arranged on his desk to facilitate this review. Before looking at them, I asked the president, "Tell me, how do you feel about your people? Generally speaking, in their spiritual qualities, are they standing on higher ground this year than they were a year ago?" I wanted to assess the president's personal discernment regarding the spiritual strength of his members. He immediately seized this opportunity to direct my attention to the reports. Sensing that he had misunderstood the intent of my question, I explained, "I will be pleased to review the reports with you, but before we do, would you tell me how you *feel* about your people?"

My insistence on his making this kind of assessment apart from the information in the reports was both frustrating and perplexing to the president. I was sensitive to his frustration, and without further discussion we went through the statistical information. It indicated considerable progress in many areas that are amenable to a quantitative evaluation. I believe the reports were significant indicators of the spiritual quality of the people. However, I had failed to draw from the president the kind of discerning evaluation I had solicited. At the same time, I sensed that he was a little perplexed and somewhat pensive at the conclusion of our interview. His pensiveness continued throughout the meetings of the afternoon and evening and caused me some concern.

On the following day, as the president delivered his address in the general session of the conference, he surprised me by telling the members about his experience with me the previous day. He acknowledged his frustration over my apparent reluctance to go into an immediate review of his activity reports, and this frustration had remained with him into the night. As he was pondering these things, there came into his mind an experience he had had during the week prior to the conference.

He had visited a member of the stake who was in the hospital recuperating from surgery. During this visit a nurse had entered the room, making her regular calls on the patients. She had gone to some charts that were hanging at the foot of the patient's bed, carefully perused the notations, and then added some of her own. She had then stepped to the side of the patient, felt her pulse, placed a hand on her forehead, asked some questions, and received some responses. The president said, "It occurred to me that the nurse was attempting to assess some of the patient's vital signs—some that were not reflected in the notations on the charts."

The president said that it was then in his reflections that the purpose of my questioning the day before had registered with him. "I realized," he said, "that Elder Larsen was asking me to assess your spiritual vital signs in ways that the reports may not have revealed."

He then continued, "Today I am going to talk with you about those spiritual vital signs—those that go beyond the information on the charts." He proceeded to give one of the finest talks I have heard a stake president give. Interestingly, in the talk he made no reference to the statistical reports.

We have good reason to feel encouraged and optimistic today as we observe the rapid growth of the Church throughout the world. We can be pleased with the level of participation of the members, even though we acknowledge that it can be improved. The willingness of the people to serve and to sacrifice for the sake of the Lord's work is commendable.

But what of the kingdom that is within our own souls? There are evidences that we are not completely free from weaknesses within. Family problems multiply. Divorce becomes more common. Signs of preoccupation with worldly, material concerns are apparent on every side. Questionable compliance with principles of trust and integrity in business dealings is too frequent. Courtesy and kindness are too often replaced by abruptness and rudeness in human relations. Growing evidences of promiscuity and infidelity to marriage covenants beset us.

While acknowledging that The Church of Jesus Christ of Latter-day Saints is the "only true and living church upon the face of the whole earth, . . . speaking unto the church collectively and not individually," the Lord expressed a reservation about the individual members as he explained, "For I the Lord cannot look upon sin with the least degree of allowance" (D&C 1:30–31).

At another time he warned those of his church: "Behold, vengeance cometh speedily upon the inhabitants of the earth. . . . And upon my house shall it begin, and from my house shall it go forth, saith the Lord; first among those among you, saith the Lord, who have professed to know my name and have not known me, and have blasphemed against me in the midst of my house, saith the Lord." (D&C 112:24–26.)

In this time of impressive Church growth it is well for us to look within our own souls to assess our individual spiritual vital signs. Too frequently Latter-day Saints of all ages yield to the temptation to explore and sample forbidden things of the world. Often this is not done with the intent to embrace these things permanently, but with the knowing decision to indulge in them momentarily, as though they hold a value of some kind too important or too exciting to pass by. While some recover from these excursions, an increasingly large number of tragedies occur that bring a blight and a despair into many lives.

The cumulative effect of this is devastating. The reverberations will affect the lives of those who indulge, as well as the lives of those who have loved and trusted them, in unfortunate and unforeseen ways for indefinite periods of time. As a consequence of these things, humanity slips inexorably to a lower level, the real power and influence in the Church and kingdom of God are diminished, and all mankind will inevitably feel the loss. Furthermore, as a collective church, we jeopardize our capacity to merit and claim the preserving and protecting blessings from the Lord.

For those who keep the trust placed in them and do not yield to the pattern of the times, and for those who have made or are making their way back from dark paths, I have the most profound admiration and gratitude. You are our shining hope. You are our real strength. You will make a significant difference in the final outcome of things. You are the last great counterforce against the evil that is engulfing the earth. God bless you for this!

As I view the days that lie ahead, I am hopeful because of the Lord's promise, and I know his kingdom will prevail, but I tremble as I read his declaration to us: "For this is a day of warning, and not a day of many words. For I, the Lord, am not to be mocked in the last days." (D&C 63:58.)

The enduring strength of the kingdom is not to be found in the number of its members, the rate of its growth, or the beauty of its buildings. In God's kingdom, power is not equated with body count nor with outward routine compliance with prescribed performances. It is found in those quiet uncharted acts of love, obedience, and Christian service which may never come to the attention of official leadership, but which emulate the ministry of the Lord himself.

It is a time for us to assess our own spiritual vital signs in those essential areas that takes us beyond the information on the charts. "For, behold, the kingdom of God is within you."

CHAPTER SEVEN

Accountability for Our Thoughts

*I*n the children's classic, *The Secret Garden*, Frances Hodges Burnette gives these observations about thoughts:

> One of the new things people began to find out in the last century was that thoughts—just mere thoughts—are as powerful as electric batteries—as good for one as sunlight is, or as bad for one as poison is. To let a sad thought or a bad one get into your mind is as dangerous as letting a scarlet fever germ get into your body. If you let it stay there after it has got in you may never get over it as long as you live. (*The Secret Garden*, Dell Publishing Co., 1987, p. 268.)

Thoughts have a great deal to do with how we live each day, whether we are enthusiastic or depressed, whether we experience success or failure, whether we are obedient or disobedient to the laws of God. Learning to control our thoughts is an essential part of our development here in mortal life. If we do not control our thoughts, they will eventually control us. There is that much power in thoughts.

Some modern behavioral scientists have indicated that the human thought process is much like the operation of a computer. The input controls the output in terms of attitude, mood, and behavior. Proverbs tells us that as a person "thinketh in his heart, so is he" (Proverbs 23:7). As a person persists in his thinking, so he will become.

We must be accountable for our thoughts. In his sermon on the mount, Jesus implied that thoughts and feelings would play a significant part in our being judged by him. He condemned those who would take the life of another being, for example, but he also warned against thoughts or feelings of anger. It was not enough to avoid adulterous acts. Jesus warned that anyone who looked upon another with lust had already become guilty of a serious sin.

In the revelation contained in section 88 of the Doctrine and Covenants the Lord describes some of the events that will accompany the ushering in of the millennial period and the summoning forth for judgment all those who have lived upon the earth during its telestial existence. Angels, according to the Lord's description, will sound trumpets to call forth those from the various time periods of the earth's history. Among the verses outlining these events is found this revealing entry: "And then shall the second angel sound his trump, and reveal the secret acts of men and the *thoughts and intents of their hearts,* and the mighty works of God in the second thousand years" (D&C 88:109, italics added).

Apparently a record is made of our thoughts as well as of our acts. Both will play a part in determining what our eternal prospects will be.

As we contemplate the necessity of controlling our thoughts, it may be well to think of our mental processes as having two compartments. This is an over-simplification, of course, but it may have some usefulness. Into the foyer or antechamber of our minds come many impulses or fleeting images that are prompted by things we see, or hear, or feel, or smell. We cannot always control the initial intrusion of these impulses with which we are bombarded. However, even as with unwelcome visitors who may occasionally seek to gain entrance into our homes, we have the power to usher out, almost instantaneously, those negative impulses that come into the antechamber of our minds. We have a responsibility to do this. No one can do it for us.

We should invite into the living room of our minds, and into our "hearts," to use the scriptural metaphor, only those thoughts that will be good for us and will prompt us to act in an acceptable way. This process requires great discipline and personal accountability. If only positive, wholesome, uplifting thought impulses are allowed to find permanent lodging in our minds and hearts, our overt behavior will probably be close to what it should be. Our relationships with others will tend to be positive and rewarding. Our capacity to deal satisfactorily with the challenges of life will be greatly enhanced.

If, on the other hand, we submit to the intrusion of demeaning, negative, destructive thought impulses, we are certain to find their ultimate effect in our lives.

Our moods and our attitudes toward daily living and toward each other are in large measure regulated by our thoughts. To a considerable degree we can control whether or not we are happy or unhappy, enthusiastic or discouraged, by the things we permit ourselves to think about. Another sentence or two about one of the principal characters in *The Secret Garden* is illustrative of this point:

> So long as Colin shut himself up in his room and thought only of his fears and weaknesses and his detestation of people who looked at him and re- flected hourly on humps and early death, he was a hysterical, half-crazy little hypochondriac who knew nothing of the sunshine and the spring and also did not know that he could get well and stand upon his feet if he tried to do it. When new beauti- ful thoughts began to push out the old hideous ones, life began to come back to him, his blood ran healthfully through his veins and strength poured into him like a flood. . . . Much more sur- prising things can happen to anyone who, when a disagreeable or discouraged thought comes into his mind, just has the sense to remember in time to push it out by putting in an agreeable, deter- minedly courageous one. Two things cannot be in one place.

> "Where you tend a rose, my lad,
> A thistle cannot grow."
> (*The Secret Garden*, p. 270.)

Sometimes we hear counsel given about devices that might be used to protect us against bad thoughts. Sing- ing a hymn or reciting in our minds some lines of poetry or verses of scripture has been suggested. Such devices may be momentarily helpful, but they represent a defensive stance only. One cannot always be on the defensive against bad thoughts. It is essential to develop a capacity for sustained positive thinking. Keeping one's mind actively involved with constructive, useful things is the best protection. An idle mind becomes a ready repository for thoughts that have a negative influence on our feelings and behavior. There is so much of good literature, music, and art, and so many constructive challenges to work through to conclusions in our minds. We can focus our minds upon only one thought channel at one time. When good actors are performing on the stage of our mind, it is difficult for the bad actors to intrude.

When I served as a mission president, I frequently spent many hours driving in an automobile from one missionary area to another. There was abundant time to think. I found it helpful on these occasions to organize gospel sermons in my mind, forming relationships among scriptural topics and developing these into a useful bank of stored material that could be drawn upon as needed.

In order to sustain constructive thinking it is necessary to have something worthwhile to think about; to have in reserve some problems or challenges that must be thought through to a conclusion. When this exercise is combined with purposeful prayer, it becomes one of the best means to tap into the power of revelation. It is hard work. It requires as much conditioning mentally as is required in a physical sense to run a long-distance race. A flabby mind cannot respond to these mental challenges any better than a flabby body can respond to physical ones.

When Oliver Cowdery had failed in his initial attempts to translate from ancient records, the Lord said to him: "Behold, you have not understood; you have supposed that I would give it unto you, when you took no thought save it was to ask me. But, behold, I say unto you, that you must study it out in your mind: then you must ask me if it be right, and if it is right I will cause that your bosom shall burn within you; therefore, you shall feel that it is right." (D&C 9:7–8.)

Sometimes it is good to engage in original thinking as we look to new ways to solve certain problems. There are those who have become walking encyclopedias of the thoughts and conclusions of others, but they have seldom had an original thought of their own. Such people contribute little to progress. They may be impressive with their wealth of stored information, but they lack a degree of creative power that is essential to dynamic growth.

One of the most compelling lessons taught in all of the literature available to us with regard to the power of thoughts is the story of King David in the Old Testament. As a young man, David demonstrated a courage and strength, both morally and physically, that is not excelled among all the great characters in the scriptures. He fought with wild beasts and overcame them, defeated the giant Goliath, and then served for many years as the leader of Israel. In all of these things he reflected unusual wisdom, control, and self-discipline. In his later years David experienced a terrible tragedy. It came not because of weakness, but because he was unwise. It seems that David had reached a point of such personal strength that he felt he could safely indulge himself in thinking about some enticing possibilities regarding the wife of one of his officers. David's thoughts overcame his strength and eventually controlled him. The consequences for David were severe. Explaining David's situation to Joseph Smith, the Lord said: "For he hath fallen from his exaltation, and received his portion." And then, with reference to David's wives and families, the Lord said: "For I gave them unto another." (D&C 132:39.)

We are free to think whatever thoughts we choose and to consider a full range of possibilities, but we are not free to choose the consequences of those thoughts. "As he thinketh in his heart, so is he."

The Savior said: "For out of the abundance of the heart the mouth speaketh. A good man out of the good treasure of the heart bringeth forth good things: and an evil man out of the evil treasure bringeth forth evil things." (Matthew 12:34–35.) "For out of the heart proceed evil thoughts, murders, adulteries, fornications, thefts, false witness, blasphemies" (Matthew 15:19).

Another interesting episode from the scriptures reflects the positive effects of good, purposeful thoughts. Enos, a Book of Mormon leader, went into the forest to hunt wild beasts. In the wild solitude of that eventful day, Enos began to think about things of an eternal nature about which he had heard his father speak. These thoughts went deep into Enos's heart, and he was prompted to reach out in earnest prayer for an understanding of his status before God. As a result, the course of Enos's life was changed. He became a powerful force for good in accomplishing the Lord's purposes. His prayers were answered in a remarkable way. (See Enos 1:1–18.)

Of the days of Noah just before the Flood, we have this description of the people: "And God saw that the wickedness of man was great in the earth, and that every imagination of the thoughts of his heart was only evil continually" (Genesis 6:5).

We are accountable for what we think. Our thought processes are such that when we submit ourselves to influences that produce thoughts, particularly those that we take into our hearts, we are fashioning the kind of life we will live, whether it be for good or for ill. There is that much power in thoughts.

As we learn to control our thought processes and take into the living room of our minds, as it were, only those things that will produce positive results in our lives, we develop an essential level of accountability. As we read in *The Secret Garden*, "Where you tend a rose, my lad, a thistle cannot grow."

CHAPTER EIGHT

Accountability for Achieving Goals

Much has been said and written in recent years about the value of goal-setting and the importance of guiding our lives toward certain predetermined objectives. This process has taken on many of the aspects of an exact science. It has found expression in the world of education in the form of behavioral objectives. In the corporate and industrial world it sometimes manifests itself in a "management-by-objective" philosophy. Some individuals feel that unless each hour of each day is programmed to achieve specific objectives, life cannot be lived to the full, and personal potential is being cheated. In fact, this general notion has become so universally accepted that to question the value of goal-setting in the achievement of any public or private enterprise is no longer rational in the general point of view.

Setting goals and objectives to guide one's efforts toward accomplishment is one of the processes of human dynamics which can be demonstrated to yield positive results. It is a process, however, which can also be restricting and limiting when it is distorted or misguided. It is important to hold this process in the right perspective when we seek an understanding of the principles which lead to human progress and to individual accountability.

An important distinction must be made between the potentially confining process of setting specific goals and objectives and the more encompassing need of having a general purpose in life. This distinction is more than a play upon words. A person's purpose in life has an overriding influence upon what he does with his time, energy, and resources. It can also have a profound effect upon how he relates to other people. Without this purpose life has no compass. Within the framework of such a purpose there is an acceptable place for much spontaneity and flexibility. Indeed, without this freedom life can become stilted and sterile, and much of the potential for progressive inspiration and renewal can be thwarted. Appropriate, useful goals and objectives must be a direct outgrowth of one's perceived purpose in life. Otherwise they can lead to a random expenditure of effort and resources that may not contribute effectively to long-range progress.

Purpose entails much that is qualitative. It does not always lend itself to quantitative measurement in terms of numbers, percentages, size, and volume. In today's material world most objectives are considered to be meaningless unless they are expressed in quantitative terms and are susceptible to measurement within these terms.

It is important for us to bear in mind that worthwhile goals and objectives can be of a qualitative nature as well as a quantitative one; that is, they can relate to the quality of people, things, and relationships as well as to numbers and size. In a materialistic society much more attention and validity seem to be attached to quantitative goals, probably because they are more easily measured and reflect more directly profit and loss, material growth, and production. This should not lead to the conclusion that attainments of a qualitative nature are less important than those that lend themselves to easy numerical measurement. In fact, in the realm of moral and spiritual things, qualities may be much more significant than quantities. The nature of one's relationship to others may have more value than his "productivity."

There is no conclusive evidence that setting and working toward quantitative objectives always produces beneficial qualitative effects in one's life. Indeed, a too-intent focus upon the acquisition or production of quantities of things may actually obscure the need for qualitative development, and in the world of spiritual things such a condition could be an obstruction to the achievement of the goals that matter most.

The material world places a high premium on quantitative things. Gross national product, profit margins, sales and production quotas, and interest rates are the substance of corporate life and death. Men and women ascend to positions of power and authority on the basis of their ability to *produce*, and on their capacity to get others to do the same. In this arena, product can easily be thought of as having greater importance than people. People can be viewed simply as a means to enhance production. Success and achievement can become product-centered. Product is measurable. Goals and objectives in this environment are generally and understandably of a quantitative nature.

Interestingly, such a focus upon attaining measurable objectives seems to generate a tendency to program production methods and procedures in order to guarantee acceptable production levels. This can apply to the attainment of sales quotas as well as to quotas of materials that flow from the production line. It can be effectively demonstrated that programming and regimentation of procedure will result in an acceptable minimum production level and thus provide a safe profit margin. Systems, processes, and programs therefore become essential in most profit-making enterprises.

Offering material incentives to stimulate sales or production is also a common practice. Competition is generally intense—competition for notoriety and power as well as for material rewards. All of this helps toward increased production. In this atmosphere of competition and struggle for preeminence, the adage "When performance is measured, performance improves" generally holds true, especially when position and compensation are at stake. When objectives can be expressed quantitatively in terms of profit and loss and when people's continued employment and promise of reward are based upon meeting these objectives, then the management-by-objective system becomes a reasonable and profitable approach to administration.

Whether this approach can be applied with equal success to the attainment of spiritual and moral qualities is open to question. Spiritual qualities do not necessarily develop in the same environment as that which fosters the attributes upon which such high value is placed in the material world, nor can they always be accurately measured in a quantitative way. This is not to suggest that qualities of the spirit are not susceptible to assessment. But they must be assessed by spiritual means. They are closely associated with feelings, attitudes, commitments, and perceptions, but they are not always easily measured in a quantitative way at arbitrarily established audit periods.

At one time Elder Adam S. Bennion drew attention to the fact that Abraham Lincoln probably saw his first slave auction at about age sixteen. While this experience undoubtedly left a profound impression upon the young man, he did not go and immediately produce the Emancipation Proclamation. The additional encounters and experiences that brought Lincoln to a position of commitment and a course of action in opposition to slavery all made their contributions to the final outcome, but their individual effect was not overtly measurable at particular points in his early life. One's assessment of what was happening in his consciousness and conviction would likely have depended upon more subtle perceptions and discernment.

The same is so often true of one who experiences conversion to the principles of the gospel of Jesus Christ. This conversion process can be a lengthy one. It can have a profound effect upon one's purpose in life. But its progress cannot always be accurately assessed by measurable performance at arbitrary points in time.

Those who attempt to measure qualitative growth with a quantitative measuring system of necessity must look for a "product." This product generally takes the form of some overt behavior or performance which can be counted and evaluated numerically. The frequency or regularity with which the performance is given can be taken to be a direct reflection of the quality of commit-

ment possessed by the individual who is being measured. Those who rely upon this kind of assessment
often submit to the temptation to program for specific
kinds of measurable performances, presumably related
to the qualities desired in the individual. These performances are taken to be a direct evidence of internal commitment and conviction. Since the numbers or percentages now "produced" by the responsive individual
become the prime measuring rod of devotion, the tendency increases to program and regiment specified
kinds of behavior so that the numbers or percentages
will look good. Those who devise the programs and the
prescribed activities must now demonstrate their success on the basis of the numbers produced.

In this process the importance of people and their intrinsic qualities can easily become subverted to the need
for their production of measurable data. If the data is
good, the people are presumed to be progressing quali-
tatively as well. The thesis which produces this system
requires that this conclusion has validity. Unfortu-
nately, there is much of history and experience to prove
that the system does not always work. Inevitably it has
produced discrepancies and distortions. Such was the
case with the children of Israel under the law of Moses.
Outward performance, that which the apostle Paul referred to as the "works of the law," became the primary
objective.

One of the most difficult challenges for the Apostle
Paul and other missionaries in the meridian of times was
the unyielding loyalty of the converted Jews to the
ritualism and outward performances of the law of
Moses. Even those who accepted Christ and became
baptized members of his church had great difficulty in
relinquishing their ties to the law. Apparently, many of

them insisted on perpetuating, even after baptism, the programs and practices which had been developed over many years by the Jewish religious leaders. Some of them insisted that gentile converts to the Church also adopt the practices of the law of Moses. Obviously, they attached an efficacy to these performances and rituals that they could not easily discard.

Their insistence on perpetuating these things within the new Church was a constant source of concern for Paul. It was even an occasional cause for discord and misunderstanding among Church leaders, as Paul indicates in his letter to the Galatians (see Galatians 2:11). There is evidence in the book of Acts that some Christian Jews followed in the footsteps of Paul and his missionary successes, attempting to convince Paul's converts that they must now adopt the programs of the Jewish law as well as the principles of the restored gospel. This led to a major controversy in the Church and precipitated a general-level leadership conference in Jerusalem which Paul attended to represent the views of the gentile Saints.

The account of this conference, which is contained in the fifteenth chapter of Acts, is most revealing. It discloses the intense loyalty that many Church leaders still felt toward the programs and procedures of the old law. This loyalty was obviously an outgrowth of a deep-set conviction on the part of some Church leaders that the "works of the law" were essential to salvation and that individual progress and perfection could not occur without a strict observance of the rituals. After "much disputing" at this conference, Peter made an attempt at a compromise that would free the gentile converts from adherence to the provisions of the law, but which apparently would allow the Jewish Christians to continue their old practices if they chose to do so. While Peter's recommendation was accepted by this conference, it is apparent that the issue was not settled. Adherents to the practices within the law of Moses continued to press for an acceptance of their position. Years later, when Paul visited Jerusalem once again, he encountered the same controversy (see Acts 21:17–24).

This loyalty to and affinity for programs that were an outgrowth of the ritualism and regimentation of the past proved to be a great obstacle in the way of accepting the simple, basic principles that the gospel of Christ provided. For the converted Jews, whose lives had been so filled with the programmed requirements of the law and whose religious commitment had been demonstrated by their outward observance of these requirements, the religious life outlined by the gospel of Christ must have seemed very open and unregulated. It was not easy for them to leave the feeling of security provided in the total regimentation of the Jewish law. Obviously, they could not understand how the gentile Saints could possibly be trusted to develop any of the qualities prescribed by the new beliefs without the same set of regulations and procedures to guide them and fill up their lives.

As the Savior confronted this same problem among the Jews, he not only decried the meaningless machinations which the law had imposed upon them but he also blamed this outward ritualism for having crowded out of their lives the qualities of virtue, charity, and compassion that were so important to the life plan that he reintroduced. He accused the Pharisees and scribes of fostering this hypocrisy. "Well hath Esaias prophesied of you hypocrites, as it is written, This people honoureth me with their lips, but their heart is far from me. . . . For laying aside the commandment of God, ye hold the tradition of men, as the washing of pots and cups: and many other such like things ye do." (Mark 7:6, 8.) He accused them of being like whited sepulchres, impressive in their outward show, but inside full of dead men's bones and all uncleanness (see Matthew 23:27).

It appears that the Savior was not only concerned with the unproductive expenditure of effort required by the programmed processes of the law but was also alert to the inevitable diversion away from the development of the important inward qualities of life that are so essential to salvation.

Paul attacked this same problem in his great admonition to the Corinthian Saints on the subject of charity (1 Corinthians 13). To the Galatians who had begun to experience the freedom offered by the gospel of Christ, Paul said: "Stand fast therefore in the liberty wherewith Christ hath made us free, and be not entangled again with the yoke of bondage. Behold, I Paul say unto you, that if ye be circumcised, Christ shall profit you nothing. . . . For in Jesus Christ neither circumcision availeth any thing, nor uncircumcision; but faith which worketh by love." (Galatians 5:1-2, 6.)

There is sometimes the danger that the true purpose of an endeavor can be lost in the compulsion to make the records look good. As an example of this, I cite an incident related to me by a young wife who had just gone through the trauma of losing a baby through premature birth. Throughout the month of semi-confinement that preceded the misfortune, members of the Relief Society in this sister's ward made frequent calls on her to comfort her, to bring meals for the family, and to be of general assistance. Their caring concern and attention had been much appreciated.

Following her release from the hospital, this sister deeply felt the need to spend some private time with her scriptures and in prayerful quest for understanding. She reported that on a day at the close of the month she was at home alone, particularly impressed and inspired by some part of the scriptures she had been reading. A sweet spirit of peace and consolation rested upon her, and she felt a closeness to the Lord and the reality of his love in a way she had never experienced before.

She was absorbed in this experience when the telephone rang. She reluctantly answered, only to find that it was one of the Relief Society sisters who had been in her home several times earlier in the month. On this occasion the call was to solicit a time during the day when an official visit could be made to present the lesson for the month. When the sister who related this incident to me asked to forego the lesson in view of the fact that the visiting teachers had already been in her home several times during the month, and more especially because she did not wish to have her restoring interlude with the scriptures interrupted, she was reminded that this was the *last* day of the month. On the earlier visits the official lesson for the month had not been presented. Therefore, the visits could not be counted.

Reluctantly, the ailing sister left her scriptures and cleaned her house in preparation for the visit of the visiting teachers. The spirit of the morning was lost and was replaced by a feeling of resentment and hurt. The visiting teachers' perfect record remained intact—but at what cost?

As members of the Church and human beings in general reach for a higher level of moral and spiritual attainment, they will be required to more clearly define the principal purposes in life. They will need to be motivated more toward the qualities of life associated with this kind of existence than toward the quantities of things they can produce or acquire. Historically the

Lord's people have always achieved their highest levels in material acquisitions as a by-product of their attainment of high spiritual and moral qualities. It has never occurred in reverse order as to time sequence or as to priority.

Goals and objectives within the framework of life's true purpose can be helpful in motivating and in maintaining general direction. The more important of these will be of a qualitative nature, and their achievement must be evaluated more by discernment and observation than by quantitative measurement. In such an environment the doctrine of the priesthood will distil upon the people as the dews from heaven. Whatever dominion is achieved by man over himself or over material things will not then come by compulsion but as a natural and inevitable result of his having qualified for such an endowment. (See D&C 84.)

CHAPTER NINE

Freedom to Act
Has Its Consequences

We are greatly privileged to be upon the earth during a time when so much culminating activity is going forward in preparation for the Lord's return. Our participation in these activities and events provides us with unique opportunities and obligations.

It is likely that no other event in the history of the earth will match the splendor and the consequence of the Lord's appearance in his glory to reign upon the earth. It will be the grand, fulfilling climax to the earth's telestial life. In order for the work of the millennial period to be accomplished, some dramatic changes will occur in the condition of life upon the earth. This is a time of preparation for that day. It is a time of peril for those who are not giving obedience to the commandments of the Lord.

There have been other such times in this earth's history, which may give us some indication of the circumstances into which we are moving. In Noah's day life had become so corrupt that the Lord determined to make a new beginning. The account in Genesis tells us: "And God saw that the wickedness of man was great in the earth, and that every imagination of the thoughts of his heart was only evil continually. The earth also was corrupt before God, and the earth was filled with violence. . . . for all flesh had corrupted his way upon the earth." (Genesis 6:5, 11–12.)

To Noah, the Lord made this declaration: "The end of all flesh is come before me; for the earth is filled with violence through them; and, behold, I will destroy them with the earth" (Genesis 6:13).

In order that he might preserve those who would be obedient to him in Noah's day, God sent prophets among the people to warn them of the forthcoming calamity. In doing this he set a pattern which he has followed in other similar circumstances. Among these prophets was Enoch. To him the Lord said: "Enoch, my son, prophesy unto this people, and say unto them—Repent, for thus saith the Lord: I am angry with this people, and my fierce anger is kindled against them; for their hearts have waxed hard, and their ears are dull of hearing, and their eyes cannot see afar off" (Moses 6:27).

As in other times with other prophets, there were those who responded to Enoch's inspired warnings. They were preserved in an island of righteousness among the sea of filth and violence and corruption which swirled about them. "And the Lord called his people Zion, because they were of one heart and one mind, and dwelt in righteousness" (Moses 7:18).

Prior to the deluge that ultimately swept the earth, the Lord took Enoch and his people to himself in a dramatic transfiguration. Of them the account says simply: "And lo, Zion, in process of time, was taken up into heaven. And the Lord said unto Enoch: behold mine abode forever." (Moses 7:21.)

The Lord has never unleashed destructive forces upon the earth for the purpose of cleansing without warning the people in advance. Always they have been given ample opportunity to repent so that they might be preserved. Nephi acknowledged the Lord's mercy in this regard when he said: "And as one generation hath been destroyed among the Jews because of iniquity, even so have they been destroyed from generation to generation according to their iniquities; and never hath any of them been destroyed save it were foretold them by the prophets of the Lord" (2 Nephi 25:9).

It is typical of the people of the earth prior to these cleansing periods that they viewed themselves as quite secure and free from threat. They ridiculed the warnings of the prophets. We are told that in the days of Noah the people continued their riotous living, eating and drinking, marrying and giving in marriage, right up to the time the Flood came.

This was true also of those who lived upon the American continent just prior to the Savior's appearance for his brief ministry among the Book of Mormon peoples. Prophets had gone among the people warning of the cleansing that was to come. Samuel, the Lamanite prophet, foretold the portending destruction in great detail. Signs and wonders were shown to the people so that they would repent. The account says: "Nevertheless, the people began to harden their hearts, all save it were the most believing part of them . . . and began to depend upon their own strength and upon their own wisdom, saying: some things they [the prophets] may have guessed right, among so many; but behold, we know that all these great and marvelous works cannot come to pass, of which has been spoken. And they began to reason and to contend among themselves, saying: that it is not reasonable that such a being as a Christ shall come." (Helaman 16:15–18.)

We know of the great destruction that came upon the Nephite-Lamanite peoples in America. Only the more righteous part of the people were spared, as the Lord had promised.

We live in a time much like Noah's, and very much like that of Samuel, the Lamanite prophet. Just as in those earlier periods, the promises of the Lord that pertain to our day are open and available to us. They are plain and easily understood. Of our day the Lord has said: "For a desolating scourge shall go forth among the inhabitants of the earth, and shall continue to be poured out from time to time, if they repent not, until the earth is empty, and the inhabitants thereof are consumed away and utterly destroyed by the brightness of my coming. Behold, I tell you these things, even as I also told the people of the destruction of Jerusalem; and my word shall be verified at this time as it hath hitherto been verified." (D&C 5:19–20.)

As tides of evil engulf the earth, as they did in the days of Noah and the time of the ancient inhabitants of America, the Lord has given to us his true gospel, that we might save ourselves and that we might be a beacon to all who are not content to be swept along with the current of wickedness. Millions of people upon the earth are uneasy with their circumstances. Many are anxiously looking for an anchor of truth and security. Of them President Spencer W. Kimball said: "There are numerous people in the world who are hungering for the

Lord and his word. They are thirsting for association with the Lord, and yet they neither know exactly what they are hungry for, nor what will quench their thirst."

In these times of urgency and peril, the Lord has placed great trust in us. He expects us to be the city on the hill, the salt of the earth spoken of by the Savior. We must be able to demonstrate in our lives the benefits of living in obedience to the truths of the gospel of Christ. He expects the fruits of the gospel to be visible in our lives so that others may be attracted to its principles of truth. He has said, "Arise and shine forth, that thy light may be a standard for the nations: and that the gathering together upon the land of Zion, and upon her stakes, may be for a defense, and for a refuge from the storm, and from wrath when it shall be poured out without mixture upon the whole earth" (D&C 115:5-6).

On another occasion he said: "For Zion must increase in beauty, and in holiness; her borders must be enlarged; her stakes must be strengthened; yea, verily, I say unto you, Zion must arise and put on her beautiful garments (D&C 82:14).

And again: "For, behold, I say unto you that Zion shall flourish, and the glory of the Lord shall be upon her; and she shall be an ensign unto the people, and there shall come unto her out of every nation under heaven" (D&C 64:41-42).

President John Taylor saw our day and said:

> We have got this kingdom to build up; and it is not a phantom, but a reality. . . . And now, you may write it down, any of you, and I will prophesy it in the name of God. And then will be fulfilled that prediction to be found in one of the revelations given through the Prophet Joseph Smith.

Those who will not take up their sword to fight against their neighbor must needs flee to Zion for safety. And they will come, saying, "We do not know anything of the principles of your religion, but we perceive that you are an honest community; you administer justice and righteousness, and we want to live with you and receive the protection of your laws."

Will we protect such people? Yes, all honorable men. When the people shall have torn to shreds the Constitution of the United States, the Elders of Israel will be found holding it up to the nations of the earth and proclaiming liberty and equal rights to all men, and extending the hand of fellowship to the oppressed of all nations. (*Journal of Discourses* 21:8.)

We have much more than our own lives and our own preservation to be concerned about. The Lord expects much of us. As the world drifts once again into iniquity, he expects those of us who have received the truth to demonstrate the advantages of the gospel way of life in such a manner that all honest people will be drawn to his church and kingdom through us. This will not be a flamboyant public relations effort to gain notoriety. It will come from the aggregate effect of lives lived in obedience to gospel truths, from honest dealings with our fellowmen, from neighborliness and friendliness, virtue, benevolence, and long-suffering. It will likely come less from preaching and more from worthy example. The Savior said: "Let your light so shine before men, that they may see your good works, and glorify your Father which is in heaven" (Matthew 5:16).

If we do not live in obedience to the gospel, we betray the trust that has been placed in us. It is not enough to be concerned about the welfare of our own souls. We must be obedient for the sake of those millions of people who are looking for a refuge. The more we look, and act, and think like the world, the more difficult we make it for honest people to recognize the advantages of following the Lord's way. Whenever we cheat or lie or compromise our virtue to any degree, we fail in our trust. Whenever we make ourselves like the disobedient of the world in our appearance, in our fashions, in our music, in our talk, we fail in our trust. We become as salt that has lost its savor and is thenceforth good for nothing but to be cast out.

This is a gravely serious matter. The Lord will not be mocked in these things. We have the freedom to choose our own course of action, individually and as a people, but we are not free to determine the consequences. The Lord has made that perfectly clear. Speaking of the members of the Church in this dispensation, the Savior has said:

"For behold, and lo, vengeance cometh speedily upon the ungodly as the whirlwind; and who shall escape it? The Lord's scourge shall pass over by night and by day, and the report thereof shall vex all people; yea, it shall not be stayed until the Lord come. Nevertheless, Zion shall escape if she observes to do all things whatsoever I have commanded her. But if she observe not to do whatsoever I have commanded her, I will visit her according to all her works, with sore affliction, with pestilence, with plague, with sword, with vengeance, with devouring fire." (D&C 97:22–23, 25–26.)

Do we believe the Lord means what he says, or do we

reason and excuse ourselves as did the people before the Flood and as those who lived on the American continent before the Savior's ministry there? Can the words of the Lord be any more plain? Of the great cleansing that will occur in our time preceding the Lord's return, he says:

> Verily, verily, I say unto you, darkness covereth the earth, and gross darkness the minds of the people, and all flesh has become corrupt before my face.
>
> Behold, vengeance cometh speedily upon the inhabitants of the earth, a day of wrath, a day of burning, a day of desolation, of weeping, of mourning, and of lamentation; and as a whirlwind it shall come upon all the face of the earth, saith the Lord.
>
> And upon my house shall it begin, and from my house it shall go forth, saith the Lord;
>
> First among those among you, saith the Lord, who have professed to know my name and have not known me, and have blasphemed against me in the midst of my house, saith the Lord. (D&C 112:23-26.)

We rejoice today in the rapid growth of the Church throughout the earth, and well we should. But what about the Church and the gospel in our individual lives? Are we maintaining our distinctiveness from the iniquitous world? Are our families free from divorce? Has fornication and adultery been removed from among us? Are all of our young people marrying in the Church and in the temples? Do all of us pay our tithes and offerings? Do we keep the Sabbath day holy? Do we have clean thoughts? Are we upright and honest in all our dealings? Are our hearts upon the things of God's kingdom rather than upon the material things of the world? Is love and peace and harmony increasing in our homes? Do our testimonies carry the power born of obedience?

These are perilous times. The promises of the Lord are as irrevocable and sure in our day as they have been hitherto. He has not left us to wonder or to reason or to speculate. His language has been plain and direct. This is a day of preparation. The Lord has said, "If [Zion] sin no more none of these things shall come upon her" (D&C 97:27).

This is a time to take stock of our own lives. If there is need for repentance, we must take the necessary steps, not only for our own sakes but also for the sake of those who are yet looking for the truth and who need to see it reflected in our lives. Inconsequential as the rise of the Church may have seemed to many in the world, it will yet stand supreme. As the systems and governments contrived by men fail—and they will—the Church and kingdom of God will emerge as a bulwark of freedom and justice for the righteous of all nations. The parable spoken by the Savior to his disciples will then be fully understood: "The kingdom of heaven is like to a grain of mustard seed, which a man took, and sowed in his field: which indeed is the least of all seeds: but when it is grown, it is the greatest among herbs, and becometh a tree, so that the birds of the air come and lodge in the branches thereof" (Matthew 13:31–32).

Joseph Smith made this significant observation:

Even Jesus, the Son of God, had to . . . restrain His feelings many times for the safety of Himself and His followers, and had to conceal the righteous purposes of His heart in relation to many things pertaining to His Father's kingdom. When still a boy He had all the intelligence necessary to enable Him to rule and govern the kingdom of the Jews, and could reason with the wisest and most profound doctors of law and divinity, and make their theories and practice to appear like folly compared with the wisdom He possessed; but he was a boy only, and lacked physical strength even to defend his own person, and was subject to cold, to hunger, and to death. So it is with The Church of Jesus Christ of Latter-day Saints; we have the revelation of Jesus, and the knowledge within us is sufficient to organize a righteous government upon the earth, and to give universal peace to all mankind, if they would receive it, but we lack the physical strength, as did our Savior when a child, to defend our principles, and we have of necessity to be afflicted, persecuted, and smitten, and to bear it patiently until Jacob is of age, then he will take care of himself. (*History of the Church* 6:608–9.)

The warning and the promise given by the Lord to ancient Israel applies perfectly to us today. He warned:

But if ye will not hearken unto me, and will not do all these commandments;

And if ye shall despise my statutes, or if your soul abhor my judgments, so that ye will not do all my commandments, but that ye break my covenant:

I also will do this unto you; I will even appoint over you terror, consumption, and the burning ague, that shall consume the eyes, and cause sorrow of heart: and ye shall sow your seed in vain, for your enemies shall eat it.

And I will set my face against you, and ye shall be slain before your enemies: they that hate you shall reign over you; and ye shall flee when none pursueth you.

And if ye will not yet for all this hearken unto me, then I will punish you seven times more for your sins.

And I will break the pride of your power; and I will make your heaven as iron, and your earth as brass:

And your strength shall be spent in vain: for your land shall not yield her increase, neither shall the trees of the land yield their fruits.

And if ye walk contrary unto me, and will not hearken unto me; I will bring seven times more plagues upon you according to your sins.

I will also send wild beasts among you, which shall rob you of your children, and destroy your cattle, and make you few in number; and your high ways shall be desolate. (Leviticus 26:14–22.)

But while it is well to remember the warning, it is vitally important to keep in our minds and hearts the promise:

If ye walk in my statutes, and keep my commandments, and do them;

Then I will give you rain in due season, and the land shall yield her increase, and the trees of the field shall yield their fruit.

And your threshing shall reach unto the vintage, and the vintage shall reach unto the sowing time: and ye shall eat your bread to the full, and dwell in your land safely.

And I will give peace in the land, and ye shall lie down, and none shall make you afraid: and I will rid evil beasts out of the land, neither shall the sword go through your land.

And ye shall chase your enemies, and they shall fall before you by the sword. . . .

For I will have respect unto you, and make you fruitful, and multiply you, and establish my covenant with you. . . .

And I will walk among you, and will be your God, and ye shall be my people. (Leviticus 26:3-7, 9, 12.)

Anciently the Lord revealed to the prophet Enoch the circumstances of our day.

And the Lord said unto Enoch: As I live, even so will I come in the last days, in the days of wickedness and vengeance, to fulfill the oath which I have made unto you concerning the children of Noah;

And the day shall come that the earth shall rest, but before that day the heavens shall be darkened, and a veil of darkness shall cover the earth; and the heavens shall shake, and also the earth; and great tribulations shall be among the children of men, but my people will I preserve;

And righteousness will I send down out of heaven; and truth will I send forth out of the earth, to bear testimony of mine Only Begotten; his resurrection from the dead; yea, and also the resurrection of all men; and righteousness and truth will I cause to sweep the earth as with a flood, to gather out mine elect from the four quarters of the earth, unto a place which I shall prepare, an Holy City, that my people may gird up their loins, and be looking forth for the time of my coming; for there shall be my tabernacle, and it shall be called Zion, a New Jerusalem.

And the Lord said unto Enoch: Then shalt thou and all thy city meet them there, and we will receive them into our bosom, and they shall see us; and we will fall upon their necks, and they shall fall upon our necks, and we will kiss each other;

And there shall be mine abode, and it shall be Zion, which shall come forth out of all the creations which I have made; and for the space of a thousand years the earth shall rest. (Moses 7:60–64.)

May we be prepared for the time of cleansing that is to come, for if we are prepared, we need not fear.

Index